Arguments for a Theatre

Howard Barker

Arguments for a Theatre

Howard Barker

JOHN CALDER : LONDON
RIVERRUN PRESS : NEW YORK

First published in Great Britain, 1989, by
John Calder (Publishers) Ltd.,
9-15 Neal Street, London WC2H 9TU.

and in the United States of America, 1989, by
Riverrun Press Inc
1170 Broadway,
New York, NY 10010

British Library Cataloguing in Publication Data

Barker, Howard, 1946-
Arguments for a theatre
I. Title
792'.01
ISBN 0—7145—4152—4

Printed in Great Britain by Delta Press, Hove.
Typeset at Oxford University Computing Service.

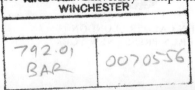

Contents

Introduction

Do we have the theatre we want? Do we have the audience we want?

What is the meaning of 'we' in those two questions?

By what rights do 'we' 'want' anything? On whose terms? In whose interests?

The definitions inherent in these questions would be re-examined and reassessed constantly as part of the pulse of a vital culture. But it is hard to find any current debate of culture which carries through to ideas being tested in practical action, and even then the appeal and value of art—particularly drama, "The Public Art"—tend to be defined and dominated by reference to an image of "The Public", a monolithic restriction and distortion of possibilities, evoking characteristics such as habitual expectations and limited abilities in confronting depth, range, effect, change. Those who work in the theatre without conscious cynicism often feel constricted, compromised, even insulted, by having to diminish their engagement of efforts for this Procrustean spectre of "The Public". Some audiences and potential audiences do too, as theatre workers and audience members must have some human traits in common, surely?

Why? On whose terms? In whose interests?

Because drama is The Public Art, and it is usually implicitly interpreted as The Art of Solidarity. But—leapfrogging usual, implicit interpretations—what if a theatre located its aesthetic in addressing what lay beyond solidarity? Not everything that is 'public' can be identified as 'an act of solidarity' except by the most strenuous ideologue. 'What we have in common' is often invoked as our greatest sense of hope. The differences between us might be sources of hope, discovery and creativity also.

Theorists of drama, including Artaud and Brecht alike, make much of the submergence of the individual sensibility and ego into a salutory corrective and/or relief provided by being united in a communal charge of feeling/thinking, the deliverance up of self to the reviving rush of instinctive entrancement or to the instruction of the greater yet humbler (because apparently anonymous) collective and its historical will. Such rhetoric of drama resembles that of sexual mystics who view the orgasm as a release from self rather than as a moment of profound self-consciousness. There is also a common implicit prescription of the sacrifice of the right to self-determination in the drama which "takes you out of yourself" only to return you to the same essential shape, except more amused/enlivened/politically correct by virtue of this temporary release from the troubling complexity of individuality.

Howard Barker's drama centres on rupture, both external and internal, and the licensing of thought and feeling, instinctive expressions of human potential amidst its ubiquitous, often self-willed, restrictions. The writings collected in this volume are speculations towards a theatre in which audience members might be neither dismayed at, nor fearful of, the public expression or illumination of discrepancies between their reactions and those of their fellow audience members—and, indeed, discrepancies between their own reactions and their sense of what is commonly, socially right as a response, even perhaps what is right as their specific individual response. In this way, the theatre becomes a site of individual discovery, demonstrating the self's capacities for surprising moments of both intransigence and realignment. The unfamiliar permission of response, and the cowed, reflexively unified response it often provokes, is illustrated by this quotation from Barker's 1987 play

The Europeans, where the Emperor addresses his courtiers:

> Sometimes you will want to laugh. And you will
> feel, no, I must not laugh. Sometimes you will
> suffer the embarrassment of one who feels exposed
> to an obnoxious privacy. You will feel, he should
> never have shown me that. And sometimes you will
> experience the terrible nausea that accompanies an
> idiocy performed by one for whom you felt respect.
> As if the world had lost its balance. I can only tell
> you, all these feelings I permit. So laugh when the
> urge seizes you, and then, be ashamed of the laugh.
> The Emperor only acts the insecurity of all order.
> Do you accept the truth of that?
> (**They shift uncomfortably**)
> No one understands! Nihil comprehensa!

Indeed, audience individuals at a Barker play might find
themselves capable of responses which are surprisingly
shameless, as well as surprisingly shameful. Later in the
same play, the Emperor proclaims the disturbing *aperçu:* '**No
moment of unity is ever true!**' (He is, of course,
profoundly untrustworthy. So are all the voices surrounding
him.) Alexander Leggatt identifies 'A fragmented world in
which values are uncertain and the individual has to
construct artificially a sense of his own identity—these are
some of the basic conditions of Shakespearean tragedy'[1].
They are also basic conditions of Barker's catastrophism,
which directly addresses the separateness of self in the
breakdown of consensus. Barker has not characterised this
separateness as necessarily to be feared, in defiance of
populist sentiment of various hues and of attempts to ignore
the breakdown of shared values and assumptions (as Jim
Hiley has indicated, 'Liberal pundits don't like to be
reminded of the collapse of the liberal consensus'[2]).

Julian Hilton has implored of drama, 'If formal innovation is to succeed, it will have to break with the classical
architecture of beginning, middle and end, as advocated by
Aristotle, but also with the episodic theatre of the Brechtian

3

kind. It must permit the possibility of moral and political meaning, but not depend on, or be circumscribed by, any single ideology'[3]. The rationalism—or more precisely pseudo-rationalism—so ingrained in twentieth-century British drama has impeded this innovation, remaining self-delightedly hypnotized by what Dragan Klaić has identified as 'the argumentative surface of rhetorics of conviction'[4], rather than being doubly disruptive of convention in both its address to unconscious and subconscious human drives and in its relationship between form and content (where form *becomes* content in experiential terms)—these are uncomfortable, because unfamiliar, directions for a drama striving beyond the dominant situation of the artist—self-consciously "political" or not—and the audience seduced into pandering to expectations they have of each other, by way of the usual, implicit interpretations of The Public Art.

Barker's ambition to strive beyond past or present relationships between theatre and audience has led him to articulate and develop his own theories of how innovation might indeed occur, setting new terms for drama criticism and exposing the ludic regressions in the terms of the criticism currently written about him and others, with a view to advancing the argument; this collection aims to provide a concentrated focus and instrument of leverage to this effect.

In contrast to the confirmatory celebrations and deterministic didacticism which dominate and atrophy contemporary theatre, Barker has rejected the reducible "message" and, increasingly, the linear narrative, in favour of cumulative effects, variations on themes and contradictory experiences which rupture familiarities and conventional pieties to permit the release and range of the imagination. Incongruities, shifting identities, unpredictable events, with the disturbing power of a newly-forged myth, enfused with the power of dream or nightmare—phenomena which are 'held together by connections which are emotionally powerful but logically inconsistent. Like life'[5]—or perhaps more like it than the omniscient air of pseudo-rationalist theatre, and with deeper and more persistent resonance. These are means by which form might, indeed, *become* content in experiential terms.

Barker's increasingly complex sense of character locates opposites which exist within each figure, so that there is no such thing as a stable character—any more than a stable audience, by implication; and Barker insists on exposing these contradictions, whatever confusion of conventional expectations (such as 'identifiable authorial viewpoint' or 'identifiable single message') results. His protagonists push their selves as far as they will go, no matter what the opposition or the awful discoveries entailed; his audiences are offered the chance to participate in, and extend the discoveries depicted.

The sub-title to Barker's 1986 play *The Bite of the Night*— 'An Education'—is a particularly felicitous choice, were one to interpret the process of education, not as systematic instruction or indoctrination, but rather as the challenge and development of intellectual, emotional and moral faculties: generating active thought in audience individuals rather than prescribing what they should think. This interpretative distinction between objectives is crucial in the evaluation of art and education alike. If only in this sole respect, one might make a connection between Barker's drama and Theatre-in-Education, another mode of drama intrinsically committed to the right of each audience member to work through and take away something different from the event, working through a method that is 'essentially heuristic', raising questions in the minds of its audience members that 'encourage them to reach for a change in their understanding', emphasising 'redefinition rather than celebration'[6]. Elliot Eisner's distinction between educational objectives is salient here: 'instructional' objectives 'specify skills and information to be learnt'; 'expressive' objectives identify a situation in which audience members 'are to work, a task in which they are to engage: but it does not specify what they are to learn... An expressive objective provides [both actor and audience member with] an invitation to explore, defer or focus on, issues that are of peculiar interest or import... An expressive objective is evocative rather than prescriptive'[7].

Numerous Barker characters lecture, expound and digress, challenging the audience to listen and follow. The protagonists of the monologues *Don't Exaggerate* and *Gary Upright* are the starkest illustrations of this, but it is also significant that Savage in *The Bite of the Night* is a professional lecturer whose activity has been legitimised personally and dramatically by his one remaining student Hogbin, one of Barker's equally numerous pupil or acolyte figures, who frequently voice probable audience unease or incomprehension at the teaching that is afforded[8]. For all the unequal power, both need and want the other as well as resisting them, testifying to Barker's recurrent interest in the dynamics of mutual challenge, and the paradoxical processes involved in forcing another into a position of autonomy, instilling a hunger which might oblige them to become their own invention: a theme analogous to Barker's own dramatic practice. Also, renegades like Gary Upright, Sordido in *Women Beware Women* and Starhemberg in *The Europeans* challenge by maintaining that others are imprisoned in mind-forged manacles to some extent of their own choice and making; and if attempting to engineer their self-release involves the renegades taking human icons like Bianca and Katrin to the edge of madness or destruction, then they appear prepared to do so, attacking individual happiness or gratification at its juncture with social equilibrium, indicating a painful, terrifying freedom which might lie beyond conciliation. These renegades take it upon themselves to involve others in agonizing confrontations with the bars of their figurative prisons; but it is the prisoner who has to choose to walk out through the ruptured door, and to embark upon their own programme of harrowing self-determination.

My suggestion of affinities between expressive educational objectives and Barker's theatre is not negated by his statement 'I have nothing to teach anyone'; in fact, he provides a startling correlation of patronising, placatory attitudes in the assertion 'We are afraid of our own audience, as a poor teacher is afraid of the class' ('Honouring the Audience') and refines the terms of the encounter: 'Rather the plays invoke moral crises which deprive the audience of its usual judgemental opinion' ('Dialogue'). But beyond disruption, the plays also encourage the audience to reach for change, however difficult, in their understanding. This encouragement is generated by witnessing 'the doing of the undoable'—a challenge which occurs on two levels. Firstly, on the level of witnessing Barker's dramatic characters undergo or submit to changes which defy our expectations or imaginings of what might be possible or conceivable for them to incorporate—and yet witnesses that incorporation occur, not only convincingly but compulsively; and secondly, on the level of witnessing Barker's actors undergo or submit to changes, in the course of representing these characters, which defy our expectations or imaginings of what might be possible for them or any actor to incorporate—and yet witness that incorporation occur, not only convincingly but compulsively. The sceptic might dismiss the occurrence of the first phenomenon as the barren fantasy of a romantic imagination, were the incontrovertible occurrence of the second not capable of achieving breakthrough, by which the occurrence of the first might be sensed as analogously, imaginatively possible. No wonder that some of Barker's most loyal and successful supporters and promoters have been actors; few dramatists issue such challenges, requiring such demonstrations of the paradoxical triumph of their craft, exploding and regenerating the configurations which, at any given moment, constitute 'human potential'.

The actor and director Ian McDiarmid, who has had a long and close association with Barker's work, asserts: 'So many actors, by the time they are asked to play the great parts, are encased in such self-protecting armour that they are no longer equipped to play them. They lack the breath and the breadth. Instead of embracing the part, they find a

7

way of keeping it at arm's length, of avoiding playing it. It is wrong for an actor to contain a part, he must open himself to all the facets the part contains. The central dynamic is to be found in the collision of the contradictions'. McDiarmid's comments on playing Shakespeare are also pertinent to playing Barker: 'Naturalistic techniques are not appropriate... The plays aim for a distillation of life, not an imitation of it. Naturalism, or theatrical behaviourism, as it may more properly be labelled, is a formula, guaranteed to rob words of their value, to limit the actor's means of expression and deny those who people the plays their essential humanity and hence their universality. The act of acting is itself the articulation of an intellectual and emotional response. Therein lies its vitality'[9]. Rather than as a minister of solidarity, McDiarmid regards the actor as an 'archetypal outsider' who 'disrupts harmony and confuses morality'[10].

Similarly, so many audiences, instead of embracing play or performance, find a way of keeping it at arm's length, of avoiding engaging with it; similarly, so many directors, and critics. Thus, actors, audiences, directors and critics collude in a self-compounding spiral whereby intellect and emotion are continually displaced by trivialising witticisms. Bernard Shaw's reflection on his days as a theatre critic remains enragingly pertinent: 'When my moral sense revolted, as it often did to the very core, it was invariably at the nauseous compliances of the theatre with conventional virtue'[11]. Thus is bred a theatre of insecurity, which lionizes conventional values for the attempted reassurance of those confined to perpetuating them, in an attitude of willed myopia.

On the other hand, the event of theatre might be the surprising confluence of various parties searching for knowledge, in their own ways, on their own terms, and finding themselves empowered to make new imaginative discoveries. Brian Bates: 'Personal knowledge leads to power. But it is not a power to dominate and control others, which stems from personal insecurities. Rather, it is the power to direct one's own destiny in the face of pressures to lead a life defined by the well-rutted channels. While the supposed aims of scientific psychology are to "predict and control human behaviour", the way of the actor aims at self-understanding, which may render the person *less* predictable and controllable by outside forces... The way of the actor adds nothing to our lives. Rather it *takes away;* blocks, restrictions, fears, boundaries and conventional views of the self and experience'[1][2]. However, it is worth adding that this demolition of the habitual adds, at least, new challenge; demands a reach of want to surge into the vacuums created by the demolished self-restrictions, and thus the process of self-redefinition begins, on the shoulders, as it were, of the drama witnessed.

Barker has emerged, unique in his generation and country, as an aesthetic-existentialist theorist who dares to match the disturbing power of Wilde, Nietzsche and Sartre, and dares to develop both classical and revolutionary ambitions into speculations towards new theatres, new cultures. Beyond even this, his drama and poetry work in an arena, and towards an aim, of his own making and constant remaking: specifically, the soundings of profound personal difference by a central series of images or initiatives; and the very exploration of change, the dynamic which rips people out of their former selves, more alive but raw and bleeding, and impels them into a journey through uncharted territory where things and persons are constantly on the verge of turning into their supposed opposites: one's act of courage and faith might strike another as a bolt of the most profoundly painful evil. These collected philosophical epigrams and essays are pursuits of enquiry, challenging the theatre to anticipate its own identity, discover its creativity in new terms which might oppose their very existence to habitual associations, presented circumstances and the constraint of imagination by imposed status: arguments for an as yet non-existent theatre, which would thrive on arguments *in* the theatre as a manifestation of vitality, a mortar of change, beyond fear or shame. Rather than be stifled into mute or laughing inertia by deference to the

9

myth of The Public, which has displaced courage from the centre of most theatres (On whose terms? In whose interests?), participants in the theatre which Barker envisions might separately express or discover disunity which, when publicly emblazoned, becomes beautiful and terrible, excessive and frustrating, wounding and splendid. Here, contrary visions of purity are necessarily and permanently at war with each other, as are different levels of self-knowledge and hope. Here, polarisations fracture, stability dissolves, and love and ruthlessness co-exist in the same person, in the same action. Authority and profanity split open against each other, exposing, in each, both fears and anticipations of possibilities of regeneration.

1. *English Drama: Shakespeare to the Restoration, 1590–1660* (Longman, London, 1988), 59.
2. *The Listener,* 15 September 1988, 42.
3. *Performance* (Macmillan, London, 1987), 152.
4. Conference on Terrorism and Politics in Modern Drama, 4–10 September 1988, IUC Dubrovnik.
5. Brian Bates, *The Way of the Actor* (Century, London, 1986), 136–.
6. Charmian C. Savill, 'Theatre-in-Education in Wales', *Planet* 67 (Feb–Mar 1988), 49–54.
7. Quoted by Tony Jackson in *Learning Through Theatre,* ed. Tony Jackson (Manchester University Press, 1980), 77.
8. Other examples in Barker's canon are Downchild and Stoat in *Downchild,* Gaukroger and Pool in *Pity in History,* Toplis and Music in *Crimes in Hot Countries,* Sordido and both The Ward and Leantio in *Women Beware Women,* Lvov and the disciples in *The Last Supper.*
9. 'Shylock' in *Players of Shakespeare 2,* ed. Russell Jackson and Robert Smallwood (Cambridge University Press, 1988), 47.
10. *Ibid,* 54.
11. *Three Plays for Puritans* (Penguin, London, 1946), 13–14.
12. *Op.cit.,* 9, 202.

*49 Asides for a Tragic Theatre**

We are living the extinction of official socialism. When the opposition loses its politics, it must root in art.

The time for satire is ended. Nothing can be satirised in the authoritarian state. It is culture reduced to playing the spoons. The stockbroker laughs, and the satirist plays the spoons.

The authoritarian art form is the musical.

The accountant is the new censor. The accountant claps his hands at the full theatre. The official socialist also hankers for the full theatre. But full for what?

In an age of populism, the progressive artist is the artist who is not afraid of silence.

The baying of an audience in pursuit of unity is a sound of despair.

In a bad time laughter is a rattle of fear.

How hard it is to sit in a silent theatre.

There is silence and silence. Like the colour black, there are colours within silence.

The silence of compulsion is the greatest achievement of the actor and the dramatist.

We must overcome the urge to do things in unison. To chant together, to hum banal tunes together, is not collectivity.

*First published in *The Guardian,* 10th February 1986.

11

A carnival is not a revolution.

After the carnival, after the removal of the masks, you are precisely who you were before. After the tragedy, you are not certain who you are.

Ideology is the outcome of pain.

Some people want to know pain. There is no truth on the cheap.

There are more people in pursuit of knowledge than the accountants will admit.

There is always the possibility of an avalanche of truth-seekers.

Art is a problem. The man or woman who exposes himself to art exposes himself to another problem.

It is an error typical of the accountant to think there is no audience for the problem.

Some people want to grow in their souls.

But not all people. Consequently, tragedy is elitist.

Because you cannot address everybody, you may as well address the impatient.

The opposition in art has nothing but the quality of its imagination.

The only possible resistance to a culture of banality is quality.

Because they try to debase language, the voice of the actor becomes an instrument of revolt.

The actor is both the greatest resource of freedom and the subtlest instrument of repression.

If language is restored to the actor he ruptures the imaginative blockade of the culture. If he speaks banality he piles up servitude.

Tragedy liberates language from banality. It returns poetry to speech.

Tragedy is not about reconciliation. Consequently, it is the art form for our time.

Tragedy resists the trivialisation of experience, which is the project of the authoritarian regime.

People will endure anything for a grain of truth.

But not all people. Therefore a tragic theatre will be elitist.

Tragedy was impossible as long as hope was confused with comfort. Suddenly tragedy is possible again.

When a child fell under a bus they called it a tragedy. On the contrary, it was an accident. We have had a drama of accidents masquerading as tragedy.

The tragedies of the 60s were not tragedies but failures of the social services.

The theatre must start to take its audience seriously. It must stop telling them stories they can understand.

It is not to insult an audience to offer it ambiguity.

The narrative form is dying in our hands.

In tragedy, the audience is disunited. It sits alone. It suffers alone.

In the endless drizzle of false collectivity, tragedy restores pain to the individual.

You emerge from tragedy equipped against lies. After the musical, you are anyone's fool.

Tragedy offends the sensibilities. It drags the unconscious into the public place. It therefore silences the banging of the tambourine which characterises the authoritarian and the labourist culture alike.

It dares to be beautiful. Who talks of beauty in the theatre any more? They think it is to do with the costumes.

Beauty, which is possible only in tragedy, subverts the lie of human squalor which lies at the heart of the new authoritarianism.

When society is officially philistine, the complexity of tragedy becomes a source of resistance.

Because they have bled life out of the word freedom, the word justice attains a new significance. Only tragedy makes justice its preoccupation.

Since no art form generates action, the most appropriate art for a culture on the edge of extinction is one that stimulates pain.

The issues are never too complex for expression.

It is never too late to forestall the death of Europe.

*Ye Gotta Laugh**

I

We grew ashamed of the I in the theatre and learned to talk of the We. Rightly, because the art is collective, and because we were doing new things, rapidly making enemies.

I also wanted to belong, and found at once the actors were the allies who knew by speaking what struck and what missed better than the managers, who are careerists or idealists, or writers, who follow each other.

I sensed the authority of the spoken word but still did not grasp its range, its arc of effect in a culture frantic with images, fevered with pictures and products, visually sick.

The word was deliberately maimed, pulped into headline or spewed into naturalistic loops. Speech, as art, was spattered with a double contempt, by the left who required workers to grunt and the right, who were coming to the masses at last, levelling princesses to the suburban mode.

When the politics broke, the We was lost in the tide. The culture, nakedly cannibalistic, lent authority to despair, made a ground for archaic theologies and permitted philistinism to parade as democratic art.

The managers leapt to sham renaissance postures, wanting power, gold, and spectacle, while the fringe, which had sheltered even those whose aesthetic was not oppositional, suffered a double relapse, a miniaturist art no longer fitting the ambition of writer or actor and shrivelling again into scenes of domestic life.

*'Ye Gotta Laugh' was commissioned for an unpublished collection of essays. The title is the refrain of the clown McGroot from 'The Power of the Dog'.

2

I did not wish for a theatre of despair, but I experienced despair. I wrote as a title, *Scenes of Overcoming,* thinking I might overcome myself. I wrote also, *Choices in Reaction,* thinking of the choices I might myself have.

I always knew socialism was tragedy. I had represented it as tragedy early on, in *Fair Slaughter.* I had repeatedly studied its failure. But in the breaking of the politics of the time, I needed to know what meaning socialism had for me. I risked finding it had no meaning. It was no use repeating the catechisms. It was futile to rest a theatre on given things.

I found it possible to begin the play without socialism but to find socialism within the play. So the audience had to share my not knowing, when it was accustomed to being taught. I was in any case exhausted by certainty itself.

So the audience was sometimes angered, being used to the autocracy of the author, the Brechtian absolutism. I no longer wanted to tell the audience anything but to invite their participation in a hunting down of tolerance.

Consequently, I became less satirical, and satire had been one of my foundations, a skill I brought with me to the theatre, ready-made. But to be a satirist, you must know, and I knew less and less, not as an affectation (the conventional wisdom of diminishing knowledge) but through practical work in character.

The deterioration of habitual moral and political assumptions was the sole means by which a change in form became possible. This was inevitable at a time of political collapse. But the resistance had to lie in questions of first principle, which is the theatre's special territory. For example, our participation in acts of violence.

3

I wrote epic plays which commanded long entrances. I set my theatre in landscapes, not because I secretly wished to write film, but because the Polish swamp or the Flanders plain were manifestations of consciousness, just as the castle in *The Castle* is not set but the outcome of spiritual despair, and the burned out gaol in *The Hang of the Gaol* a massive shade of frustrated longing. But the Kremlin had to be implied by two plywood steps (*The Power of the Dog*) and the castle was shouted into place. Always the actor and the designer were flogged into substitution. This poverty of resource bore another corruption, which was to make it common belief the work was somehow remote, and the audience non-existent. The idea of the stable audience is a reactionary one, a blunt weapon used against the revolutionary text. It is a notion of the people used against people, and the sing-song of the populist state. The cultural managers will demonstrate the frivolity, the absence of concentration, the impatience, the dictatorship of television habits over the minds of the audience, but never the appetite for challenge, truth, or discrimination. The Public, as an invention, becomes the enemy of the artist, a solid bloc of immovable entertainment-seekers whose numbers and subsequent economic power forbid intelligence. I refused this as a description of the audience and the description of myself as a problematical writer. I found, in collaboration with actors and directors, the audience for the work, sometimes half-hostile, but wanting. The tension between the audience and the play became for me an aesthetic, the nature of experience. This involved challenges to common morality, common socialism, even what passes for common humanity. So the theatre became for me a ground for assessment and potential reconstruction.

4

We make a fetish now of contradiction. We make banality of the discovery that the personal and the political do not sit, that socialism has violated as many as it has liberated, that the masses oppress as well as suffer, and that the individual is both an imperialist of the soul and the entire focus of freedom. And the contradictions pile upon each other in the Populist State. We find quality to be revolutionary, discrimination subversive, unanimity a spiritual poverty and the intelligentsia flinging its wits away, clambering through the decomposing heap of video and pop star's bones that constitutes monetarist art. The surge of the Populist State, applauded by the left in one of its basest cultural spasms, medievalizes us, teaching us that literacy leads nowhere, that plague comes over the hill, from the Ukraine or Cumbria, and to fuck with strangers is to dice with death. All these contradictions we artistically rejoice in, finding it a sort of freedom, for the new man Brecht would have engineered is anathema to us, a mechanical proletarian cosmonaut, horribly unafraid. Our problem is to reach beyond contradiction, towards the ground of tragedy. If the legitimate incredulity which is our reaction to so much planned social disintegration is summed up in the refrain of Archie McGroot at the court of Joseph Stalin, 'Ye gotta laugh, no, ye gotta laugh!' (*Power of the Dog*) then the task of serious art is to describe not wickedness but collusion, not simply authority but submission.

5

I gnawed at English socialism for ten years (from *Claw*, through *A Passion in Six Days,* to *Downchild*), coming at last to History, which is where I had begun, neither official history nor documentary history, whose truth I deny, but the history of emotion, looking for a politics of the emotions. I discovered that the only things worth describing now are things that do not happen, just as the only history plays worth writing concern themselves with what did not occur. New writing began at the Royal Court with the description of things that were not seen, (i.e. real life). Writing now has to engage with what is not seen (i.e. the imagination) because real life is annexed, reproduced, soporific. The political play showed what is, but the reaction to what is has been only laughter, and through laughter, acquiescence. The political play must now return the onus to the audience, to the soul. A theatre which dares to return the audience to its soul, which has been seen by the left for so long as given, material, finite, oppressed, will experience the hostility a wrecked ship feels for the gale.

6

The individual must be denied the sanctuary of class.

The form of the play must reflect not its ability to report certain truths which at times cannot be told elsewhere, which renders it news, but its distinctive quality as form, which is the living actor, who cannot be confused with real life.

Everything is possessed except the imagination. We have laboured through a theatre whose naturalism has consigned imagination to the same dustbin as fantasy.

The task of theatre is not to produce cohesion or the myth of solidarity but to return the individual to himself. Not, 'We must act!' but 'Are we thus?'

It is a simple task to persuade an audience of a character's evil. The important task is to persuade the audience of its potential or actual participation in evil.

A moral theatre is not one which separates the sheep from the goats (the exploited, the exploiter) but accuses the exploited also.

Plays are much too short. The manager likes the short play, it fits his wage bills. The writer of short plays thinks 'they will grow impatient with me!' Because truth is complex, art is also complex. It cannot be smashed to fit the timetable of trains.

One day a play will be written for which men and women will miss a day's work.

It is likely this play will itself be experienced as work.

7

I came to theatre ignorant of almost every classic text and with half a dozen matinees behind me. I came to it because I could write speech and was impatient with novels, but also because it existed and clamoured for big and little texts, lunchtimes, studios, events. But for many years I could not justify my being there at all. I could not find any but the most instinctive motives for art of any kind. 'I had to...' 'I needed to...'. So self in motion seemed sufficient cause. But there seemed something shameful in using so public a medium for a private end, so I invoked my socialism, and talked of 'opposition', thinking I helped a class, or at best, was testament. Later, I found in the study of the artist himself (*No End of Blame, Scenes from an Execution*) the cause that was neither wholly self nor the rattling egotism of entertainment, (which I also owned, but was suspicious of). This was a sense of artistic responsibility both to order and to violation, on the one hand to the language and the literary culture which was equipment only a fool tossed away, either out of wrong opposition or false solidarity with the uneducated, and on the other, to the furtherest reaches of speculation whether of desire or dissolution. I found the greatest moments in theatre were the most ambiguous, and truth, a thing we now hardly dare invoke, came only by excellence of the performer grinding on the complexity of text, and when it worked, worked against the will.

Conversation
with a Dead Poet*

Middleton: You are an irresponsible optimist. You have deprived the audience of its right to moral satisfaction. Admittedly you have provided a violent conclusion, but with only one murder, when I wrote five or six. I do think this is an encouragement to bad morals.

Barker: What I have done is to insist on the redemptive power of desire, opposing your view on the inherent corruptibility of all sex. Livia is a much greater character than you allowed her to be. In any case, it is simply unrealistic to inflict slaughter on all the participants in the interests of morality. It was quite obvious to me you did not believe in that yourself but were fulfilling a convention.

Middleton: I wrote for an authoritarian Christian society. Authoritarian but not philistine. The King had just authorized a translation of the Bible. You inhabit an authoritarian society, but a philistine one. James the First did not think it silly to be an intellectual. He liked universities. I understand your government is closing them down. But yes, the ending is conventional. I had the censor to think of. Yet I believe the characters got what they deserved.

Barker: What attracted me to your play when Max Stafford-Clark, Artistic Director of the Royal court, offered it to me was its obsessive linkage between money, power and sex. I saw the Florentine rulers as a rapacious class, vulgar

*Published in *The Times*, 6 February 1986 under the title 'The Redemptive Power of Desire', on the occasion of the performance of Barker's version of 'Women Beware Women'.

and not very patrician. The Duke is characterized by cupidity.

Middleton: I knew very little of Florence. But we had to situate our politics at a distance. Otherwise you could end up in prison. How do they punish you now? By taking the theatres away? It is much simpler.

Barker: England in this era is a money and squalor society, also. The connections were obvious. And money in your text corrupts everyone, though it appears to be sex that does it. I think you were only half-aware of this. Bianca is obviously seduced by the duke's wealth, not his body or his mind. And yet she immediately falls in love with him, the sexuality catching up with the acquisitiveness. The psychology of this is profound. It made me wonder what Bianca's sexuality consisted in. So I made her ask those questions, too, at a moment of terrible crisis. It launched my entire version. People start to ask, what is desire? What does it make me do?

Middleton: Your misfortune is that you have no notion of sin. Look how you have vandalized the Cardinal. You effectively remove the moral spokesman from my play, and replace him with a voyeur, a voyeur notwithstanding his intellectualism.

Barker: His speeches were conventional homilies for which a modern audience could have no sympathy. We still have writers who lecture the audience. Arguably a play is a lecture, but it must come at them obliquely, they are trained in suspicion. For us the question of the private morality of princes, or bankers, is not of the first importance, though it is hard to resist exposing it. The question for us is whether we should tolerate the deforming social effects of bankerdom itself. The sin of the false god. So I made Livia see that her life, most of which is behind her, had been rendered futile by her class affiliations. I always insist people can be saved.

Middleton: And I insist they are lost, that they have nothing but their instinct for survival. Leantio is my greatest character, a type new in my time, commonplace in yours. A middleman for merchants, he puts his love of his career even before passion. While he's absent on business, he loses his wife. Then he tries to lock her up like a piece of silver. That is a man! But, when he is robbed, he knows how to take the next opportunity. Money comes with a lecherous old woman, and he's bought!

Barker: You call Livia lecherous. She conceived an appalling desire, perhaps.

Middleton: It kills, her, anyway.

Barker: The solution to so much corruption can only be mass-murder, people falling down trap-doors and so on. It is as if you threw up your hands on human beings and wished them to hell.

Middleton: That is where they are bound for. And in case you condemn me as a cynic, remember it was I who wrote Leantio's "Canst thou forget/ The dear pains my love took, how it has watched/ Whole nights together in all weathers for thee…?".

Barker: But it cannot endure. There is always perdition at the end of it.

Middleton: As night follows day.

Barker: Contemporary reactionary ethics would make such a viewpoint welcome. We are reviving a medieval social theology in which human nature is deemed incurably corrupt in order to reconcile the poor with poverty, the sick with sickness, and the whole race with extermination. Now also money is violent, but the torturer is the accountant. We require a different form of tragedy in which the audience is encouraged, not by facile optimism or useless reconciliation, but by the spectacle of extreme struggle and the affirmation of human creativity. Failure is unimportant, the attempt is all.

Middleton: This would explain your redemption of the low-life characters. Sordido in your version is a lout with a mission, and the Ward a study in pain. I think you are even more Christian than Shakespeare dared to be.

Barker: I did no more than lend them a status you suggested yourself.

Middleton: How?

Barker: By giving them so much wit. You could not resist giving them the gift of sarcasm. They are both wonderfully bitter at the expense of posturing women, and Sordido is the obvious ideal opponent for the Duke. I pushed the *nouveau riche* flavour of your Florence, its vulgarity and accompanying poverty, into a cultural match for England now. Sordido is a model of modern youth, culturally embittered, a redundant genius who lives the life of the gutter. I massively extended the social range of your original by this one development.

Middleton: A final remark. How do you justify your continuing use of my title? What it means is my version is clear enough, but in yours?

Barker: In yours, a woman engineers the fall of a woman, for a man. That is the role of women in your time. In mine, a woman engineers the fall of a woman, but for her own enlightenment. But the pain is terrible. So the title finds an irony it never had in your play.

Middleton: May I congratulate you on assembling such a distinguished company of actors to perform this monstrous assault on the canon of English literature? It suggests to me that now, as in my time, the more ferocious the imagination, the more loyalty it commands.

On Language in Drama*

I would like to discard at the beginning of this paper any argument about drama's responsibilities towards naturalism or what passes for authentic speech. The defence of obscenity on the grounds that it is prevalent in the street is not one which interests me or seems specially legitimate. I have never been interested in reported speech or the reproduction of authentic voices. Only those writers and producers who claim to reflect life-as-it-is-lived are saddled with the contradiction of deleting expletives and sexual nouns whilst claiming to address people in their own tongue.

I would prefer rather to make a few points about the dramatist's responsibility to a higher truth than mere authenticity. The drama which I practise creates its own world, it does not require validation from external sources, either of ideology or of spurious realism, which is itself an ideology. It is compellingly imaginative and without responsibility to historical or political convention. The audience is made aware of this very rapidly—within a scene or two it is invited to discard its normal assumptions about the manner in which reality is reproduced. What is signalled is the appearance of different dramatic values and what is witnessed is not the reiteration of common knowledge but a dislocation of perceptions—in other words, it is engaging with a work of art in which the normal criteria of offence and empathy are abolished. I would stress

*Given as a paper at the BBC Seminar on Obscene Language on 14th June 1988 and subsequently published in the *Independent* on 20th June, 1988 under the title "Irreplaceable Words".

criteria of offence and empathy are abolished. I would stress that this is nothing at all to do with entertainment, which is perfectly able to operate within a limited vocabulary for the simple reason that it operates within a limited range of emotions. A tragic drama exposes the entire range of human emotions and attempts to extend it, and it entails an obligation to explore, describe and speculate on all areas of human experience. Language is the means by which emotion is conveyed—in radio almost entirely so—and the two or three words we are so often exercised about are among the most highly charged in the vocabulary. Because of the responsibility of drama to emotional truth, these words cannot simply be abolished. The bland question so often put to writers, 'Do you really need those words?' rings with a false innocence. The hidden meaning of this question is 'Do you really need those feelings?' and attempts to restrict vocabulary are invariably attempts to restrict emotion. The words are irreplaceable for the reason that they are charged with a combined fear and longing. It is not for nothing that the word 'cunt' operates both as the most extreme notation of abuse and also the furtherest reach of desire, and not only in male speech, and in attempting to eliminate the word the thing itself is eliminated, since nothing can stand in for it. Since what cannot be expressed cannot exist dramatically, the attempt to abolish the word becomes an attack on the body itself—a veiled attempt to remove the body from dramatic space. The debate about words becomes a debate about the body, who owns it, and who describes it, and if the words are forbidden to the artist, the body reverts to the doctor. I would suggest that the aim of the language censor is to return the body to the biology class where eroticism is displaced and desire corrupted into a squalid fetishism. Furthermore, I would propose that those who seek to inhibit emotion in drama through the concept of obscenity betray a contempt for the audience. The false notion of a guardianship of values is in effect a bid for moral engineering.

I am a writer who has and still does make conscious use of words conventionally described as obscene. I use them with

27

calculation and discrimination for their dramatic effect. I place the words in the mouths of certain characters sometimes abusively, sometimes erotically, and sometimes with calculated excess, and always with the deliberate intention of creating the unease in the audience which is for me the condition of experiencing tragedy, an unease which is at the opposite pole from the apathy an audience feels in a state of entertainment. Drama, as I suggested above, is not life described but life imagined, it is possibility and not reproduction. The idea of obscenity is related to shame, and shame can be both employed and overcome by the fullest commitment of the actor and writer to the emotion described, to its validity and truth, and where this occurs the initial frisson of discomfort experienced by the audience in the presence of an actor arguing the body is replaced by an awe for the powers of human emotion. In this way the obscenity becomes a ground for moral revaluation.

Radical Elitism in the Theatre*

Most theatre managements, literary departments and directors would claim to be liberals, and class, gender, sexuality, violence, iconoclasm and blasphemy have all been welcome on their stages. There is only one sin left, and it is identified as Elitism, a sin for which the left and right share an obsessive contempt, and consequently, it is a sin with compelling attractions. I would like to say a few things about sinning in the contemporary theatre, about sinners in art, and how I came to be one.

Like most fallen souls, I never meant it. I intended to be cruel, and witty, and in the old-fashioned sense, realistic... So I described what I knew, and after one short play, I had no more to add. I achieved a promising debut, but I sensed in the vaguest way I had not employed my imagination at all, I had merely reported on conditions. I was never to become a Royal Court writer. To articulate the profound dissatisfaction I felt took me a number of years. All I had to go on was a sense of opposition. I now know that what I wanted was a licence to speculate in a theatre that was resolutely naturalistic, and the courage to dream in a medium which had become reverential towards journalism and consequently, crucially documentary. This genre, of course, had its political gestation. In the post-war period identified around 1956, the bourgeois intellectuals who dominated and continue to dominate the theatre located

*Given as a paper at University of Cork, 21st November, 1987, and subsequently published under the title 'The Possibilities', Plays and Players, March 1988.

not only the progressive, but also the sexual and the vigorous, in the working class, but being class-constructed themselves, took an essentially pessimistic view of the class's potentialities. Principally, they believed it lacked imagination. They wanted to know it, but only in forms they themselves constructed, principally, the theatrical form of naturalism...

To an extent Fifties naturalism, and Sixties political theatre were reactions against an effete and pseudo-poetical theatre which had surfaced after the war, a theatre whose anaemic rhythms and sham history made the thirst for an art closer to the life of "ordinary people" more extreme. The headlong rush towards documentary theatre, which reached its apotheosis in the methods of the Joint Stock Theatre in the 1970s, sanctified research and the collective, emphasized 'relevance' as socially useful, and diminished the authorial identity. The writer remained the chief constructor of the play, but the onus was upon him to employ experienc gained in collective work by the company, and the primacy of the message could not be concealed. The emphasis remained largely what it had been throughout the Fifties and Sixties—the exposure of living conditions, the exposure of capitalist rackets, the deprivation of classes. There is little ambiguity in the Royal Court play of the last 25 years, other than that surrounding the circumstances of its production.

In common with other writers I had made attempts on the naturalistic play by a number of means. Firstly, satire, secondly, in my case, by the effective banning of the room. There are rooms in my plays but they are peculiar rooms, rarely domestic and usually varieties of torture chambers... There are gymnasiums, banquetting halls, castles, burned-out goals, but few domestic interiors. Unconsciously, I was resisting the reconciliation that the home enforces, for behind all domestic drama lies the spectre of reconciliation. Once the walls were taken down and the home abolished, imagination was liberated and speculation became possible. I was however, blocked from further progress by the very device which had initially released me from the naturalistic theatre: Satire. The ease with which I could switch to a satirical mode is obvious from nearly any text. Tragedy, which was the only route, was effectively blocked by this recurrent impulse. A very good example of this is *The Power of The Dog,* which opens with a scene in which Churchill and Stalin divide the world, the Yalta meeting. So grotesque was the politics enacted at this moment in history that I could neither view it objectively nor discover a tragic form for it. The inescapable baseness of power broking on this scale commanded a satirical response, and it remains perhaps the finest satirical scene I have attempted, arguably dwarfing the anti-historical scenes that make up the bulk of the play... I would argue that it is not possible to destroy your enemies by comedy. The comedy that exists in my work is a cruel one, and the laughter that emerges uneasily from it is a laughter of disbelief and not a laugh of public unity... I realized that my theatre would be about dislocation and not unification. I knew the laugh I wanted would be strained and born of a profound confusion, or as I wrote in the long poem *Don't Exaggerate* that Ian McDiarmid has so brilliantly performed, 'The irresistible collapse of words before the spectacle of unbidden truth'. I was wading into the heresy that would serve to isolate me from powerful elements in the English theatre...

The volume of massaging theatre produced by our major companies does not, peculiarly, indicate a lack of moral commitment. It is not a pure hunger for gold that has driven some of our best directors into the world of the musical. They may believe the conventional wisdom that art never changes anything, but in their hearts they are the tin crusaders of the new populism, with a positively renaissance appetite for personal gain on the one hand but a knocked-together ideology on the other. They think of an audience as something not to be trusted, as a semi-educated mass in need of protection, and protection in particular from complexity, ambiguity, and the potential disorder which lurks behind the imagination. With the end of full employment and the de-sanctification of welfare, the old liberal urge to please a morally confused and unhappy public by uniting it behind shallow collective responses became overwhelming. The conditions for the creation of Populist Theatre were all present when Thatcher took office. But the orchestration of populism was delegated to the liberal left who have, despite the apparently sweeping effects of political revolution, been left securely in office.

I must own up to the fact that even before I was identified as an artistic sinner conditions were never easy for my plays to find producers. I have described elsewhere the weary travels of my texts, and arguably the best ones suffered the longest. *Victory, The Castle, Crimes in Hot Countries, The Power of the Dog, The Love of a Good Man, Claw,* all waited years to find theatres. My major play on Helen of Troy, *The Bite of the Night,* has been abandoned by the Royal Court, who commissioned it, and has found no other home*. My play *The Europeans,* commissioned by the Royal Shakespeare Company, has been returned after a silence of nine months. The National Theatre has been offered every play of mine in the last ten years and ignored every one. And so on. I have been encouraged to join the actors Kenny Ireland and Hugh Fraser to set up a new company whose sole function is the production of Barker plays, The Wrestling School.†

A public has appeared for my theatre which does not appear to suffer offence in the way its guardians do, or more precisely, it is prepared to study its offence. In the midst of a surge in comedy and musical, a demand for intellectual intransigence has made itself apparent. This public appetite for the play of pain and problem made itself apparent during the season of my work at the RSC's Pit Theatre in 1985. The outstanding success of all the plays, but in

*Produced by the RSC at The Pit, August 1988, in a production by Danny Boyle.

†First production "The Last Supper", March, 1988, directed by Kenny Ireland.

particular, of *The Castle,* a work of unremitting harshness conventionally described as pessimistic set in the crusades but entirely free of history, was almost certainly unexpected by the theatre management. When this season sold out, no attempt was made to extend the number of performances, nor has any plan to revive them ever been proposed...

It is a characteristic of this period, and one which again reminds us that nothing is what it was, and nothing will ever be what it was again, that a government of the extreme right—if that is what it is—should base its moral status on the idea of the infallibility of the People.... The manifestation of this inside the arts is a campaign against subsidy, and this is perfectly coherent, since if the People want your art they will obviously pay for it, and if they don't, by what right does it exist? Success here as in other fields is defined by financial return. Now this is the predictable programme of any right wing populist regime. What was unpredictable however, was the extent of the collaboration in this exercise by proclaimed enemies of the right, who are the most vociferous in identifying the sin of elitism whether in the form of class-ownership of art forms, as in some opera, or in any art which might aspire to complexity, difficulty, or anything which has a literary tone, and I mean by that, the refusal of naturalistic speech and the elevation of language as the vehicle of complex articulation... It is the fate of words to pass from Heaven to Hell during the lifetime of a culture, but the degeneration of the word Elite into an item of abuse has been more rapid than most. It stands in for anything that is not popularly and instantly comprehensible...

Now there is nothing at all elitist about imagination, though few are as yet entitled to exercise it for a living. This is the privilege, but also the responsibility of artists. An artist uses imagination to speculate about life as it is lived, and proposes, consciously or unconsciously, life as it might be lived. The more daringly he dreams, therefore, the more subversive he becomes. I have already talked about a theatre of journalism, and a journalists' theatre certainly isn't elitist. But neither is it subversive. No journalist ever suggested the possibility of other life, he can only expose existing life, and existing life, which has become raised into a cult—and a reactionary cult—in the phenomenon of the soap opera, forbids the imaginative.

A further easy-to-identify characteristic of the elitist theatre is its relative silence. You may have noticed that we live in a laughing society. The sound of laughter mechanically reproduced, is the sound of this era. The status of comedians has never been higher. In my latest play, *The Last Supper,* laughter has become so artificial, so mechanical, that it has ceased to be attached to human beings at all, and drifts over the landscape like a storm cloud, discharging itself over battlefields and banquets alike... I would suggest that a theatre which takes itself seriously—and it must do if people are to take it seriously—cannot any longer afford to be comic. In a culture of diseased comedy, it can't laugh. Secondly, in an age of obsessive information, it can't afford to be factual. Facts we have in profusion, it is judgement we require. Thirdly, it must announce that life is complicated, and things are not what they seem. And fourthly, and this is why it is a radical theatre I am proposing, it must give the audience what it cannot any longer discover anywhere else—the honour of being taken seriously.

To take an audience seriously means making demands on it of a strenuous nature. There are people who wish to be stretched, challenged, even depressed by a work of art, and who will make considerable efforts to experience those things. The notion that concentration is shrivelling to forty-second spans has gained ground in a culture of kitsch television and advertising gimmickry. Boredom is produced by a failure to stimulate the imagination, and of course, kitsch is the enemy of imagination. Where imagination is stimulated, and the emotions engaged, concentration is possible for many hours. In my own theatre, great responsibility is born by the actor in luring the audience into the unknown life that exists in the text—and here you have a moment of the purest, most radical elitism—the actor's skill, the writer's invention, together release the mind of the observer from the blockage of unfreedom which is characterized in the feeling 'I don't know what this is about, therefore I reject it'. Instead the writer and the actor conspire to lure the mind into the unknown, the territory of possible changed perception... I believe in a society of increasingly restricted options that a creative mind owes it to his fellow human beings to stretch himself and them, to give others the right to be amazed, the right even to be taken to the limits of tolerance and to strain and test morality at its source.

Notes to 'The Bite of the Night'*

Social disfigurement finds no relief in the cosmetic of satire, which turns the object of scorn into an adored predator, ('Oh, his energy, oh, his ruthlessness!').

The play for an age of fracture is itself fractured, and hard to hold, as a broken bottle is hard to hold. It is without a message. (Who trusts the message-giver any more?) But not without meaning. It is the audience who constructs the meaning. The audience experiences the play individually and not collectively. It is not led, but makes its own way through a play whose effects are cumulative. The restoration of dignity to the audience begins when the text and production accept ambiguity. If it is prepared, the audience will not struggle for permanent coherence, which is associated with the narrative of naturalism, but experience the play moment by moment, truth by truth, contradiction by contradiction. The breaking of false dramatic disciplines frees people into imagination.

Beauty, which in an era of cultivated philistinism, is rare and secret, becomes a form of authentic resistance. In the theatre the restoration of beauty begins with the restoration of language.

The real end of drama in this period must be not the reproduction of reality, critical or otherwise, (the traditional model of the Royal Court play, socialistic, voyeuristic) but speculation—not what is (now unbearably decadent) but what might be, what is **imaginable.** The subject then

*First published as a programme note to a selective reading of the play, the Royal Court Theatre, 1987.

becomes not man-in-society, but knowledge itself, and the protagonist not the man-of-action (rebel or capitalist as source of pure energy) but the struggler with self. So in an era when sexuality is simultaneously cheap, domestic and soon-to-be-forbidden, desire becomes the field of inquiry most likely to stimulate a creative disorder.

The Bite of the Night is not contemporary, nor satirical, neither is it short. It is mythical, tragic and very long. It is not a play of convenience, but full of demands, on tolerance and conscience. By the use of prologues and interludes it both reaffirms ancient traditions of theatre (a place of argument and ideological war within theatre itself) and ruptures the sequential, all-knowing character of most contemporary theatre. It expects no unity of response but encourages division, and restores responsibility to the audience. Thus to sense confusion is positive, and to laugh uneasily is to discover complexity, which is our greatest hope.

Prologues to
'The Bite of the Night'

First Prologue

They brought a woman from the street
And made her sit in the stalls
By threats
By bribes
By flattery
Obliging her to share a little of her life with actors

But I don't understand art

Sit still, they said

But I don't want to see sad things

Sit still, they said

And she listened to everything
Understanding some things
But not others
Laughing rarely, and always without knowing why
Sometimes suffering disgust
Sometimes thoroughly amazed
And in the light again said

If that's art I think it is hard work
It was beyond me
So much of it beyond my actual life

But something troubled her
Something gnawed her peace
And she came a second time, armoured with friends

Sit still, she said

And again, she listened to everything
This time understanding different things
This time untroubled that some things
Could not be understood
Laughing rarely but now without shame
Sometimes suffering disgust
Sometimes thoroughly amazed
And in the light again said

That is art, it is hard work

And one friend said, too hard for me
And the other said if you will
I will come again

Because I found it hard I felt honoured

Second Prologue

It is not true that everyone wants to be
Entertained
Some want the pain of unknowing
Shh
Shh
Shh
The ecstasy of not knowing for once
The sheer suspension of not knowing
Shh
Shh
Shh
Three students in a smoke-filled room
Three girls on holiday
A pregnancy on a Saturday night
I knew that
I knew that
I already knew that

The marriage which was hardly
The socialist who wasn't
The American with the plague
I knew that
I knew that
I already knew that

We can go home now
Oh, car seat kiss my arse
We can go home now
Oh, underground upholstery
Caress my buttock
I loved that play it was so true
Take your skirt off
I loved that play it was so
Take your skirt off
What else are theatres for
Take your skirt off

This has to be the age for more musicals
Declares the manager
The people are depressed

This has to be the age for more musicals
Declares the careerist
Who thinks the tilted face is power
Who believes humming is believing

No
The problems are different
They are
They really are
I say this with all the circumspection
A brute can muster

I ask you
Hatred apart
Abuse apart
Boredom in abeyance
Politics in the cupboard

Anger in the drawer
Should we not

I know it's impossible but you still try

Not reach down beyond the known for once

I'll take you
I'll hold your throat
I will
And vomit I will tolerate
Over my shirt
Over my wrists
Your bile
Your juices
I'll be your guide
And whistler in the dark
Cougher over filthy words
And all known sentiments recycled for this house

Clarity
Meaning
Logic
And Consistency

None of it
None

I honour you too much
To paste you with what you already know so

Beyond the slums of England
Tower blocks floating on ponds of urine
Like the lighthouse on its bed of mercury

Beyond the screams of women fouled
Who have lost sight and sense of all desire

And grinning classes of male satirists
Beyond
The witty deconstruction of the literary myth
And individuals in the web of class

41

No ideology on the cheap
No ideology on the cheap

You think a thing repeated three times is a truth
You think to sing along is solidarity

No ideology on the cheap

Apologies
Old spasms
Apologies
Old temper
Apologies
Apologies

I charm you
Like the Viennese professor in the desert
Of America
My smile is a crack of pain
Like the exiled pianist in the tart's embrace
My worn fingers reach for your place
Efficiently

It's an obligation...

Honouring the Audience*

Obviously, the English theatre is in crisis. Equally obviously, its crisis reflects the crisis in the liberal intelligentsia which owns the theatre. This crisis is an intellectual one. The question, 'What kind of theatre do we want?' is best answered from the point of view of 'What kind of audience do we want?' We are in fear of our own audience, as a poor teacher is afraid of the class.

*

The word which has seeped into the vocabulary is Celebration. We do not know what to celebrate however, if only because at certain times there is nothing to celebrate. The theatre we have created celebrates nothing, though it is usually filled with laughter. Laughter appears to be a manifestation of solidarity, but it is now more often a sign of subordination. It is pain that the audience needs to experience, and not contempt. We have a theatre of contempt masquerading as comedy.

*

The liberal theatre wants to give messages. It has always wanted to give messages, it is its way of handling conscience. But no one believes the messages, even while they applaud

First published in *City Limits,* 25th February, 1988 under the title "Honour Thy Audience".

43

them. We are in a profound contradiction when the audience claps what it no longer honestly believes.

*

It is always the case that the audience is willing to know more, and to endure more, than the dramatist or producer trusts it with. The audience has been treated as a child even by the best theatres. It has been led to the meaning, as if truth were a lunch. The theatre is not a disseminator of truth but a provider of versions. Its statements are provisional. In a time when nothing is clear, the inflicting of clarity is a stale arrogance.

*

A new theatre will not be ashamed of its complexity or the absence of ideology. It will feel no obligations to lived life or to the journalistic impulse to expose conditions. It will not be about conditions at all. A theatre of conditions is a profoundly reactionary one, just as the insistently ideological is also reactionary. Like a party poster with its jabbing finger, it impels you to tear it from the wall. A new theatre will not force anyone to be free. Rather it will be an invitation to ask what freedom is.

*

A new theatre will put its faith in the will to knowledge, not knowledge given by the knowing, but the individual will to knowledge which is elicited by the experience of contradiction in the theatre. The dramatist explores the terrain, half-knowing, half-ignorant. His journey is mapped by the actors. The audience participates in the struggle to make sense of the journey, which becomes their journey also.

Consequently, what is achieved by them is achieved individually and not collectively. There is no official interpretation.

*

A theatre which honours its audience will not therefore make an icon of clarity. If a scene might mean two things it should not be reduced to one. If a speech contains its opposite it should be played for its opposites. This is not to say a new theatre will 'see both sides of the question', which is impotence and stagnation. It will rather emphasize the essential instability of character and the untrustworthiness of opinion. We need a theatre of Anti-Parable, in which the moral is made by the audience and not by the actor. Naturally, this means the parable will be interpreted differently by different individuals. A good parable should provoke an argument and not a submissive nod of the head.

*

A theatre which honours its audience permits them to escape the nightmare of being entertained, to be left hungry, because theatre is not the providing of lunch. Until the theatre is seen as something other than a soup kitchen for the rich or a doss-house for the angry it will not be honoured in its turn, for the tramp is never grateful to the charity, any more than the plutocrat respects a waiter.

*

A theatre which honours its audience will demand of its writers that they write in hazard of their consciences, for writers are paid to think dangerously, they are the explorers of the imagination, the audience expects it of them. If they

45

think safely, what is the virtue of them? Do you want to pay £10 to be told what you knew already? That is theft. Do you want to agree all the time? That is flattery, and the audience is always flattered, which is why it has become so sleek.

*

An honoured audience will quarrel with what it has seen, it will go home in a state of anger, not because it disapproves, but because it has been taken where it was reluctant to go. Thus morality is created in art, by exposure to pain and the illegitimate thought.

*

A new theatre will concede nothing to its audience, and the new audience will demand that nothing is conceded to it. It will demand the fullest expression of complexity, it will command the problem is exposed (but not solved). This new audience will demand more of the writers and the actor, and will itself set the pace of change. Only when the audience is insisting on change can the theatre be said to be in full flood. As things stand the audience is served, and its semi-conscious applause is deemed success. But genuine success is the point at which the audience, in a state of supreme seriousness, demands to be pulled further into the problem.

*

A new theatre will be over-ambitious. It will not settle for anything less than a full company of actors. The stage should swarm with life. No new writer should be taught economy, no matter what the economy demands. The new writer should be shown that the stage is a relentless space and never a room. If the new writer is taught economy the theatre will itself shrink to the size of an attic. It is probably time to shut the studio theatres in the interests of the theatre.

*

It was once believed that the writer who wrote for himself would end up speaking to himself. It was believed the writer had to write for others, i.e. using accepted practices of listening and seeing. But only the writer who truly invents for himself will acquire the audience who hungers for his invention.

*

The Politics Beyond the Politics*

In an era of authoritarian government the best theatre might learn a different function. Abandoning entertainment to the mechanical and electronic, it might engage with conscience at the deepest level. To achieve this it would learn to discard the subtle counter-authoritarianism that lurks behind all satire, and cease its unacknowledged collaboration with the ruling order by not reproducing its stereotypes. It would unburden itself of an increasingly irrelevant didacticism and evolve new relationships with its audience which were themselves essentially non-authoritarian.

How might this be achieved? A first step might be the recognition that living in a society disciplined by moral imperatives of gross simplicity, complexity itself, ambiguity itself, is a political posture of profound strength. The play which makes demands of its audience, both of an emotional and interpretive nature, becomes a source of freedom, necessarily hard won. The play which refuses the message, the lecture, the conscience-ridden exposé, but which insists upon the inventive and imaginative at every point, creates new tensions in a blandly entertainment-led culture.

The dramatist's obligation becomes an obligation not to a political position (the obvious necessity for socialism, etc., the obvious necessity for welfare, change, for kindness, etc.) but to his own imagination. His function becomes not to educate by his superior political knowledge, for who can trust that? but to lead into moral conflict by his superior

*Unpublished essay commissioned by the *Sunday Times*, 1988.

48

imagination. He does not tailor his thought to an ideology, but allows it to range freely over a landscape in which he himself should experience insecurity, exposing his own morality, his own politics, to damage on the way. In an age of unitary thought and propaganda, this is his first responsibility. He forsakes in doing so his right to tell, he is destabilised, and this produces a critical attitude in his audience, which, since it is so bred into the doctrine of messages, experiences at first the alienation felt by any public confronting a new art.

All this implies a tragic theatre. It implies the possibility of pessimism, which is wrongly associated by some with political reaction. It is a long time since my own theatre attempted acts of political instruction, though its satirical qualities always contained the hidden imperatives implicit in the form. *Victory* approached the problem of life in a post-liberal era by posing a series of accommodations, none of them respectable. Its pessimism was compensated for by its imaginative daring, its rupturing of moralities. *The Castle*'s interminable struggle between warped souls was never resolved—the play precisely lacked a politics of position—but its tragic scale, and the excoriation of feeling, lent to its audience a power to find confidence in catastrophe itself. In *The Possibilities* I recouped from a series of appalling situations a will to human dignity and complexity that came precisely from the absence of conventional politics. The unpredictability of the human soul, resistant to ideology and the tortures of logic, became a source of hope, even where death was inevitable. In *The Last Supper,* the longing for authority is shown to co-exist with a longing for its obliteration, and the play's determined refusal of the message created an uneasiness which was the sign of its relevance—neither catharsis nor epic. It is the authorial voice, straining to illuminate the blind, that prevents the proper focus of meaning in a work of art. The audience itself must be encouraged to discover meaning, and in so doing, begin some form of moral reconstruction if the politics of our time is not to become yet more narrow and intellectually repetitive. The left's insistent cry for celebration and optimism in art—sinister in its populist echo of the right—implies fixed continuity in the public, whereas morality needs to be tested and re-invented by successive generations.

The dramatist's function is now a selfish one. He must expose himself to tragic possibility by dragging into the light the half-conscious, the will to power, the will to negation, the ultimate areas of imagination which the conventional political play is not equipped to deal with. When the dramatist is himself heroic in the risks he is prepared to take with his material, his audience is honoured, and through a fog of early outrage, real changes of perception become possible. Plays of information ('how wonderfully researched!'), plays of communication ('we wish you to know the following!') are outflanked by a culture now obsessively concerned with dissemination of statistics and facts which themselves do nothing to stimulate change.

The artist's response to the primacy of fact must be to revive the concept of knowledge, which is a private acquisition of an audience thinking individually and not collectively, an audience isolated in darkness and stretched to the limits of tolerance. This knowledge, because it is forbidden by moral authoritarians of both political wings, becomes the material of a new drama which regards men and women as free, cognitive, and essentially autonomous, capable of witnessing pain without the compensation of political structures.

The Consolations
of Catastrophe*

*'Once, when I saw men with miserable faces staring at the ground,
I nutted them. In streets in Attica where I ran yobbish prior to
the war, I said cheer up you cunt and if they did not grin to order
rammed my forehead through their gristle. This was instinct but
now I see it also must be politics.'*

(*Act I, 'The Bite of the Night'*)

For some years I have been attempting to create a theatre
which lent its audience rights of interpretation. To do this
has involved transgressing in the two sacred groves of
contemporary theatre—Clarity and Realism. The text or
production which is lauded for its clarity is inevitably the
one which allows the least ambiguity, the least contradiction, and the least room for evading the smothering sense
that someone is giving you a meaning to take away with
you. It is a form of oppression masquerading as enlightenment. Similarly, the emphasis on Realism, now a term
almost defunct but still plucked like the last string of a
battered guitar, presupposes a moral weakness in the
audience, which must be presented with positive landmarks,
like posts in an estuary, if it is not to be dangerously lost in
the wastes of imagination. These dominating critical
categories are however, only potent so long as there is

*First published by *The Guardian*, 22 August 1988, under the title
"The Triumph in Defeat".

common ethical ground among artist, actor and audience. As long as the moral landscape in which theatre operated was morally coherent, whether Christian or Bourgeois-Humanist, the artist's right to exhort, elucidate and educate was unquestioned. The last decade has indicated such a deterioration of the moral consensus that it is now reasonable to ask whether even the most cherished statements of moral rectitude command a genuine assent. For example, the voluntarist statement 'It is self-evident that all men are created equal' does not, after a decade of Thatcherism and the international retreat from Official Communism, carry the same aura of authority that it once did. It requires examination, it requires to be reborn, and to be reborn, requires to be rediscovered. The function of a theatre in this climate, whose laissez-faire coolness among men points to further fractures in social morality in spite of all propaganda to the contrary, must be to return the responsibility for moral argument to the audience itself. I believe this offers the artist new opportunities but also demands of him new practices.

I have suggested that in certain states of society it is better to take nothing for granted, and a crisis in public morality provides an aperture for a new kind of theatre which I believe must locate its creative tension not between characters and arguments on the stage but between the audience and the stage itself. This theatre intervenes at an earlier point in human relations than that which it has done heretofore. The usual focus of contemporary theatre is how we live with one another on given moral predicates, ('it is bad to hurt people', 'the unfortunate should induce feelings of pity', etc.), but clearly there is now a problem with the predicates themselves. A braver theatre asks the audience to test the validity of the categories it believes it lives by. In other words, it is not about life as it is lived at all, but about life as it might be lived, about the thought which is not licensed, and about the abolished unconscious. Sympathy, and the sudden liquidation of sympathy, the permanent disruption of character, the instability of motive, are some of the means available to this project. The abolition of routine distinctions between good and bad actions, the sense that good and evil co-exist within the same psyche, that freedom and kindness may not be compatible, that pity is both a poison and an erotic stimulant, that laughter might be as often oppressive as it is rarely liberating, all these constitute the territory of a new theatrical practice, which lends its audience the potential of a personal re-assessment in the light of dramatic action. The consequence of this is a modern form of tragedy which I would call Catastrophism.

The fallacy most warmly embraced by the entertainment industry in times of moral uncertainty is the one which insists depressed peoples hunger for song and oblivion. But as many hunger for the problem to be embraced as hunger for its abolition. A theatre of Catastrophe, like the tragic theatre, insists on the limits of tolerance as its territory. It inhabits the area of maximum risk, both to the imagination and invention of its author, and to the comfort of its audience. It commands the loyalty and attention of those for whom the raucous repetition of social platitudes of both left and right appear as aridities. But the conflict experienced between the audience and what it witnesses, its exposure to the unbidden thought, creates pain and even resentment. It is distinctly not an experience associated with entertainment, and consequently an audience needs to be both prepared and, as is the case with all new theatre, educated in its own freedom. Not being conducted either by fetishisms of Clarity or Realism, it must be liberated from its fear of obscurity and encouraged to welcome its moments of loss. These moments of loss involve the breaking of the narrative thread, the sudden suspension of the story, the interruption of the obliquely related interlude, and a number of devices designed to complicate and to overwhelm the audience's habitual method of seeing. The panic which can seize an audience, oppressed by years of trained obeisance, at 'losing the thread' (as if life were a thread), whether the author's (who since Brecht has been given the status of a deity in modern theatre, the one who knows all and is permanently in command of his thoughts) or the director's (who must impose coherence at all costs) must be replaced by a sense of security in not knowing, and welcoming the same risks the author himself took in charting unknown territory, and the actors took in making the journey with maps. As Adorno wrote of the great nineteenth century novels, whose ambition the theatre must imitate if it is not to be made yet more tolerable and yet more brief, it derives its meaning precisely from the dissolution of coherent meaning.

The aim of a theatre of catastrophe in overwhelming the normal barriers of tolerance in its audience opens it to the complaint most frequently levelled at my work—the charge of pessimism. But pain and apparent defeat are not synonymous with pessimism, which is a narrow concept dear to the totalitarian mind and outlawed by the totalitarian state, where the idea of 'the depressing thought' as a threat to public morale has maimed literature and art. The nauseating cheerfulness of socialist realist literature, with its exhortations and beckonings to an impossible future, forced its practitioners to exercise their depression in private and contributed to the high suicide rate among 'progressive' artists. A similar imperative to enlighten, amuse, and stimulate good thoughts of a collective nature (family, nation, party, community) clings to the carnival mania of the left and the moral crusade of the right. But the banging of the drum is hollow and the rhetoric shallow. It is simply not credible. It is not the sum of experience. The catastrophe is also the property of the people, and it is the spectacle of human pain, of charismatic defeat, that constitutes the fascination and strength of tragedy. My own theatre has never aimed for solidarity, but to address the soul where it feels its difference. It is intended to plunge beneath the ground of common belief and to test the ground of first principles. The exhaustion felt by the audience in a theatre of this nature is not ennervating, but the imagination is stimulated and the structures of morality are tested, even if only to be affirmed. But it is the audience who must calibrate and assess. Traditional tragedy was a restatement

54

of public morality over the corpse of the transgressing protagonist—thus Brecht saw catharsis as essentially passive. But in a theatre of Catastrophe there is no restoration of certitudes, and in a sense more compelling and less manipulated than in the Epic theatre, it is the audience which is freed into authority. In a culture now so rampantly populist that the cultural distinctions of right and left have evaporated, the public have a right of access to a theatre which is neither brief nor relentlessly uplifting, but which insists on complexity and pain, and the beauty that can only be created from the spectacle of pain. In Catastrophe, whose imaginative ambition exposes the reactionary content in the miserabilism of everyday life, lies the possibility of reconstruction.

Beauty and Terror
in the Theatre of Catastrophe*

I want to discuss the idea of beauty and its political implications in some of my plays. It seems to me there are moments of graphic beauty in the staging of certain scenes and an accompanying beauty of expression, which despite the terror of the event described, or because of it, complicate and subvert the ostensible meaning. I believe this reflex in what might be called my writing personality accounts for the density of the experience and the impossibility of reducing it to fixed interpretations. I take it for granted, of course, that the play is not a lecture and therefore owes no duty of lucidity or total coherence.

I would like to take as a first example the final scene of an early play, *Claw,* which was first performed at Charles Marowitz's now defunct Open Space Theatre in 1975, and was my first 3-act play. I regarded this play at the time as a didactic play of politics demonstrating false consciousness, the futility of individualism and the myth of social mobility. The protagonist, an illegitimate war baby, defying his step-father's gnawing insistence on class-solidarity, succeeds brilliantly in his chosen career as a pimp. His activities place him in conflict with a government minister whom he numbers among his clients. He threatens to expose the man's private scandal, and misjudging his own power, finds himself incarcerated in the wing of a mental hospital which is effectively a death-chamber. Alone with his two warders, one a former assistant to the now redundant hangman, the other a turned IRA man, he senses the imminence of his

*Given as a paper at the Day School on Howard Barker, Birkbeck College, London, 10th December, 1988.

death and the absolute eradication of any trace of his existence. As a single individual, he faces obliteration for the arrogance of his challenge to organized authority. In his extremity, he appeals to the spirit of his step-father, the monotonous reciter of Marxist texts, now dead or dying in a home for the aged. The ghost appears, and exhorts him to make passionate appeal to his gaolers on the ground of their common class origin, their unarticulated proletarian solidarity, and their essential frailty in a world of brute power and manipulative politics. This speech, which is at the same time a biographical adieu, sets a tone of poetry and pity which makes a painful contrast with the environment of the death cell. Now, in a supreme effort of articulation and imagination, the redeemed pimp appeals to his killers, who hear him out with a proper consideration. The pimp completes his prayer, and in a state of exhaustion, awaits their verdict. This silence is, I suggest, the supremely beautiful moment of a play which is a journey through the stagnant pool of unlived life, soiled feeling and the moral destruction of both poverty and privilege. It is also the political climax, since it proposes to the audience the possibility of celebration, redemption and revival. As in all my plays, the antipathy felt by the audience towards an unattractive protagonist has been eroded by an intimacy of feeling accumulated over a long evening—the audience wills survival on the victim. It also wills the endorsement of the political posture of the despised parent. And it finally wills the dramatic optimism usually associated with survival. But the speech fails. The warders reach for the concealed bathtub which is to be the instrument of the hero's death. He is drowned, without resistance, on the stage. Thus the optimistic possibility is exploded—if optimism it is—and didacticism is scattered in a surge of terror.

I would suggest that despite its relative earliness as a play, this scene in *Claw* is typical of a method which characterizes my approach to the idea of political meaning. In the first place, the galloping threat of a message is annihilated by the intervention of a superior claim—that of dramatic beauty, in the same way as the potential slogan is always suffocated by the complex beauty of language delivered of its naturalistic bondage. Secondly, the visual beauty of the moment of the appeal made by the victim—his position mid-stage between two white-coated figures whose casual brutality we have at some length become acquainted with—saturates the context in which didacticism thrives. The objectification of the moment is thwarted by a complexity of emotions. Lastly, the speech itself, passionate but above all linguistically remote from common speech, even if littered with references, removes it from the realist mode. The failure of this speech, signalized not by any verbal response, but by the simple action of one of the murderers in switching on a transistor radio, is overwhelming in its horror and assuredly, in its inevitability. In one sense, the moment confirms the worst fears of the audience, that people cannot be changed, that pity is rare, that passion is always drowned in expediency. But I would now like to suggest that the context of the scene, which is one of beauty and terror, provides a political subversion of a more complex kind than the didactic form that the play at first appeared to favour. In effect, the play subverts itself, the conclusion, in its failure to project the message, obliging the audience to digest the experience in an individual way, but the beauty of the scene forbidding its extinction in the memory. The frustration of the message sets up an anxiety, while the beauty of the scene locks it in the imagination.

Claw is an early example of what I later formulated as a drama of catastrophe, but lacking the element of conquest which appears in the later plays. In other words, the protagonist does not reconstruct himself out of his circumstances. Claw, the name he elects for himself, is symbolic of violence, but never of discovery, and though he travels the breadth of society, he does not journey within himself.

In more recent plays, the substitution of beauty and terror for explicit political statement, the rejection of the expected line on a given subject, create those tensions in the audience that characterize the Catastrophic play. Tension is derived from the contradictory currents felt when wrong actions are passionately performed in pursuit of self-consciousness. I would like to take an example from my 1983 play, *Victory,* set during the restoration of 1660 and performed by the Joint Stock Company under Danny Boyle. The protagonist Bradshaw, widow of a republican intellectual, chooses to expose herself to the full blast of circumstances by abandoning her home, and, in gathering the dismembered parts of her husband's body, live a life of suspended morality. The act of collecting her husband together, futile as she discovers only in the final scene, is itself an act of extreme piety, but in doing so she consciously destroys in herself the moral habits of a lifetime. She creates a character better suited to the changed politics of the state. After months of criminal and vagrant existence, she arrives as a refugee in the London garden where Milton, the last representative of passionate republicanism, is being sheltered by a reactionary royalist. That is simply the first contradiction of the scene. The poet has been an intimate collaborator of Bradshaw's dead husband, and there is every reason to expect the two victims of the reactionary vendetta to throw themselves together and console themselves for disaster. But Bradshaw has banned this kind of reconciliation from her life. The spectacle of the blind Milton fills her with contempt, and in a surge of cruelty and mischief she strikes him across the face, deriding him. In this scene, which exemplifies the collapse of solidarity and the suspension of morality, the beauty of Bradshaw's exhilaration, her poetic recollection of lost and unrecoverable life, combined with her terroristic attack on a helpless man, serve to create a dramatic climate where political values are loosed into the air, and the audience, deprived of the predictable, is obliged to construct meaning for itself, at least until the stricken Milton, nursing his smacked face, settles the chaos in a moving, but essentially trite revolutionary catechism.

The removal of the moral climate from a scene—or, more precisely, the suspension of moral predictability—reaches a sort of apotheosis in my work in the ten short plays called *The Possibilities,* which were seen at the Almeida this year in a production by Ian McDiarmid. Each of the plays predicates a politics of oppression. In the various circumstances of the plays, historic, contemporary, theocratic or collectivist, the characters are invited to behave diplomatically, logically, or expediently by superior powers. In the one play I wish to discuss here, called *Kiss My Hands,* the wife of a radical activist inadvertently betrays her husband to his murderers, who visit their home at night. She allows them entry when they plead they have a sick comrade with them. Her husband has already thoroughly rehearsed her in the rules of not opening doors, and her lapse leads to his murder. As he is dragged away to be shot, she experiences a fit of remorse and horror, and calling her child from his bedroom, she attempts to suffocate him with a pillow, staggering over the stage in a breathless struggle whose intention is to prevent the world inflicting any further damage on his innocence. Like the moment of Bradshaw's attack on Milton, this action, in its choreography and its complete surprise, is dramatically beautiful and intellectually subversive, its power deriving from what is objectively speaking, wrong thinking. After an almost intolerable duration, the woman abandons her attempt at infanticide, recovers some degree of mental stability, and embracing her child, declares, in what must be a supreme burst of contradictory logic, that she will continue to open the door. Objectively therefore, she may be considered to be insane, since opening the door was precisely the cause of her pain. This play, like the others, offers neither advice nor instruction. It is ideologically void, and like the other two examples I have suggested, cannot be comprehended in the normal terms of political discourse. None of the three examples I have described is suggestive, nor are they manipulative of the audience in a 'realist' way, since they do not aspire to indicate 'correct' action, or 'correct' analysis. Furthermore, in their complexity and contradictory nature, they divide the audience into its individual components, a moment of fragmentation that I believe to be a significant characteristic of a Theatre of Catastrophe. This return to individual pain is unassuageable through recourse to political orthodoxy, but the power of its visual and linguistic poetry enhances the nature of the problem to an extent that denies the possibility of catharsis and creates a genuine moral anxiety. In this way, catastrophic beauty is in my view more deeply subversive than critical realism purports to be.

If a theatre of Catastrophe takes as its material the individual and the individual's ability to effect self-identification in a collective or historical nightmare, the moment of beauty is the moment of collision between two wills, the will of the irrational protagonist (the non-ideological) and the will of the irrational state (the officially ideological). In my most recent play, *The Europeans,* commissioned by the RSC but deemed unsuitable for its public, the maimed casualty of a war between empires makes public her atrocity in an attempt to prevent her pain becoming subsumed in the anodyne reconciliations which pass for public history. Refusing to permit her biography to degenerate into a statistic, she delivers the child which is one of the products of her ordeal, in a public place, struggling even against the midwives to establish the primacy of her experience over the public interest. This scene, which contains all the elements which constitute beauty and terror, is deeply unsettling, but not for the obvious reason that childbirth is rarely enacted on the stage—rather, the catastrophic enterprise of the heroine at her most assertive and irrational exposes the false content of the values that are being imposed on her, and reveals pity, reconciliation and forgetfulness as instruments of political oppression, the annihilation of individual pain in collective orthodoxy. The crucial characteristic of this, as in the other examples I have given, is that the moment of beauty is also a moment of 'wrong action'. It is precisely its 'wrongness' that is the source of its disturbance. The anxiety that is experienced as a social faux pas is here enlarged into a dramatic form, but the initially offensive nature of the action is rapidly revealed to have its own justifications in the struggle of the character to achieve some self-identification; the mother wrongly trying to suffocate her child, the tramp wrongly attacking the poet, the wilful obscenity of giving birth in the gutter. The audience, forced to re-view, re-feel, a 'wrong' action, is provoked and alerted, and launched unwillingly into consideration of morality, rather than subdued by the false solidarities of critical realism.

Juha Malmivaara's 'Scenes from an Execution', Turku, Finland, 1988

Malmivaara had failed with *The Love of a Good Man,* despite the power of his production. The audience had deserted him, walking out of the theatre. When I went to receive my bouquet, I looked out into emptiness. Malmivaara needed to prove the necessity for Barker.

He made a significant discovery. He understood that with Barker the theatre itself was a barrier to communication. He recognized that the structure of the building and its status in the community was injurious to the power of the work. The theatre-as-monument infected the audience, excluding whole groups of the community and reinforcing the commoditization of art.

He chose, instead of allowing the audience to sit in judgement on the work from the jury box of the stalls, to insist on their discomfort, which was the same discomfort experienced by the actors. He made the audience pay a price for its art by placing the production in a mile-long shed. When it saw this shed, the audience knew the conditions were different. They were prepared for the play to be different, and were obliged to suspend their instincts of judgement as well as their demands for pleasure. They knew they had forfeited their rights over the actors, and instead felt privileged to witness them. It was the actors who commanded them to see, and they crowded round each other to see better, breaking the conventions of normal witnessing. It was they who made adjustments. It was they who came as innocents to the imaginative world. Malmivaara insisted they came to art in this way, disarmed.

In one scene he placed the audience in prison with the

actor. In pure darkness he obliged them to experience at least one aspect of incarceration. Then, from a distance of hundreds of yards, the light of a lantern came. The relief of this light was a metaphor for hope. The audience trusted Malmivaara, whilst being uncertain what he would do with them next. This tension was the best condition for viewing the plays of Barker.

He knew the importance of difficulty in art and the repulsiveness of easy art. The difficulty of the text he counterpointed in the difficulty of the situation. But he did not fail to reward the audience. He gave them, above all, beauty. For their effort he rewarded them with things they had never seen before, just as the text insisted on things that had not been exposed before. He knew in theatre each production must give what cannot be reproduced in any other medium. So when the drunken sailors entered Galactia's studio, they careered from a vast distance, and their mayhem was a thing of beauty, in its music and its choreography. The audience knew this could never be witnessed again. They felt privileged. In an ordinary theatre they would have thought such things merely their due.

Malmivaara showed by this production the sacrifices audiences will make for art, the pain they are willing to share with the performers. He did not give them the simple gratifications of community theatre, with its known virtues and facile ends, but led them into deeper and deeper complexity by relieving them of the burden of prior knowledge, the burden of authority which is a barrier to new experience. He took control from them, and gave it to the actors. They dominated the audience, who were not raked above them like delegates.

Malmivaara understood that in the Barker play the audience must suspend its critical faculties and swallow the passing offence. It must give itself into the hands of the actors and delay its judgement while the play completes its journey. To achieve this he perfected a fluidity between scenes which overlaid each other, drawing the attention from place to place and emotion to emotion. He gave them no time to digest the experience, making the journey of the play a literal one. In this he approximated to the text itself, which is a river of words and images. In the static theatre the audience is gnawed by its lack of control. In Malmivaara's sheds the audience was propelled by the pace of the action and could not dwell on what it had experienced. The fatal inertia induced by the surroundings of the conventional theatre was therefore prohibited.

On Nigel Terry's Performance of Savage, in 'The Bite of the Night'*

Terry welcomed the opportunity to forfeit his own glamour. He had played so many attractive men. He had been the essence of the Romantic actor. He had played Caravaggio, Charles II, Byron, King Arthur. Now he played an unhealthy fat man whose movements were essentially comic. Terry had reached a point in his life when his profoundly curious imagination led him beyond self-consciousness, and at this moment a text appeared which was a means to his growth as a performer.

Terry experienced the journey in each performance, as any good actor must. But he found in Savage the innocence which is a crucial ingredient in evil and so brought us to fresh understanding. He saw that evil was small in its origins, and begins with insignificant mischief, even in wit. He saw that it was childish. Thus he made his audience party to his ebullience. He charmed his audience with his absurdity and was not afraid of losing face, so that his cruelty came harder on the nerves, and wounded more.

He cavorted in his moments of triumph, converting his intellectual satisfactions into physical action. In that cavorting was contained the essence of evil will. By this he demonstrated the actor's choice of significant physical expression making manifest internal states. But he did not hang his performance on the hook of his gestures. He was not corrupted by his invention. He had studied the lightness of the fat man, who is neither lethargic nor clumsy, but often dances on the tips of his toes. In this lightness he

*RSC Pit Theatre, 1988.

reached through time to the worst of the Caesars.

He found a posture in which to watch the unforgivable act. In this posture he conveyed the combination of horror and curiosity that attends all of us in the presence of pain. Eventually, this posture developed an ease, a casualness, an objectivity, which was the essence of his corruption. In the beginning he suffered the horror of parting with sympathy, and at the end, he bathed in his own indifference. Thus in this figuring of the body, he revealed the labour of his journey.

Often in rehearsal he cried out 'I don't know what I'm doing!' Angrily, he contended with the most complex motivations which were not always explicit in the text. He found these by excavating himself, by going deeper into self than actors are required to go. In the risks he took with his own conscience, he enabled the audience to forego the usual satisfactions of identification without forcing alienation upon them. He implicated them in his acts, unsettling the routine relations of actor and audience. He insisted on the humanity in inhumanity.

He controlled the language without being controlled by it. He did not allow even the moments of rhetoric to lose their thread to the character. Instead he showed the character Savage employing rhetoric as part of his own creative and imaginative world. It was not the actor Terry who became rhetorical but the character Savage indulging his rhetorical skills. But beyond this, he revealed under the performance of the rhetorician the character's will, his pain, or fear, which he demonstrated was often at variance with the content of the speech. None of this was too complex for him.

On Watching a Performance
by Life Prisoners*

In the performance they affirmed the drama as freedom. They asserted the superior life of the imagination. In the moment of performance they were not in custody.

They created character from a longing for other life. They demonstrated by their conviction that drama was a necessity and not a pleasure or a diversion.

They had committed terrible acts, which made them objects of curiosity for their audience, who were not criminals. But they obliterated their reputations by their authentic portrayal of character. They shouldered away curiosity by the power of their concentration, and made the text more fascinating than their false glamour. Their concentration was greater than the concentration of professional actors, who do not bring bad reputation with them. They outplayed the voyeur.

They had no fear of the text. They were of mixed intelligence, and little education. But they showed no humility towards language or poetry. Though they had been crushed by life, and had crushed it, they responded to the power of articulation in the text which they themselves could not achieve. They felt gratitude for the existence of speech and metaphor, and made it their own, though it was not the language of the gaol. For all their appalling experience, they ached for the deeper experience of imagination.

They did not want to act what they already knew. They

*'The Love of a Good Man', Wormwood Scrubs, 7th July 1988, directed by Alan Cormack.

had no sentiment for the naturalistic mode. They wished to inhabit other life, and felt sympathy for pain in types they had never encountered, or situations they had not dreamed. In this the gaol was overcome, even while the guard dogs barked in the yard below.

In a place which licensed no pity, they found it possible to express pity. They guarded this closely, as a privilege. They shielded it from the observation of others, who would have derided it, and exposed it only in the room which was called a theatre. So I learned that theatre was a place where feeling was permitted which was denied elsewhere.

They took the text to their cells and for months pored over it. In working the text they allowed the forbidden faculties to breathe, so that their performance was made both as actor but also as audience. In this they were unlike professional actors—the play was a substitute for lived life.

At the end of the performance they were locked in their cells, so the possibility of collective satisfaction was denied them. Alongside this play other prisoners performed a light comedy. These prisoners were not allowed to see the play. It was considered by the authorities that the bulk of the prisoners would object to the play. They would disrupt the production and might attack the actors. In a prison, the active power of morality, its coercive intolerance, is expressed most violently. The criminals, for all their bad acts, would not tolerate transgression. The gaol was thus a society as tightly regulated as the outside by relativist morality. In this society, microcosmically, theatre was perceived as an affront. What nourished some was abominated by others.

A Dialogue
with David Ian Rabey

Rabey: Lvov's assertion in *The Last Supper,* 'Only catastrophe can keep us clean', echoes Bianca's line 'Catastrophe is also birth' in *Women Beware Women,* and Starhemberg's forcible tuition of Concilia in *The Europeans.* One definition of catastrophe is the experience of living beyond the point where death is preferable to continued existence, and I wonder how close this is to your own sense of catastrophe as potential explosion of spurious notions of life's worth or purpose, opening up tormenting roads to liberation. Your characters discover capacities to perform realignments in their selves through catastrophe which are incredible even to them, the phenomenon described by Helen in *The Bite of the Night* as the human ability to lose one's mind and yet find others, to lose one's sight yet see through other channels; and these characters are purposefully disturbing in begging the question as to how self-conscious or self-aware they are in their compulsions to excavate, explicate and perform their selves.

Barker: Catastrophe in my theatre is willed, as opposed to simply endured. Bradshaw's horror at her husband's quartering is only the beginning of a journey she undertakes. Her pain is a door to catastrophic experience, which she wills upon herself, almost as if she wished to expose herself to the whole range of possible disaster, and like a piece of wood or linen, to accept the warping which hostility inflicts on her. But the fullest manifestation of catastrophe occurs in the choice Savage makes in Act I Scene I of *The Bite of the Night,* the discarding of family, the passage of sacred barriers which inhibit knowledge. This is a rupture which is made in isolation from the external. His wife, on the other hand, seizes a catastrophic opportunity with the fall of Troy to deliberately lose herself. And others also interpret bad fortune as a concealed escape, for example, Bianca's reluctant acknowledgement of meanings attaching to her own ordeal, and a forced examination of her own sexual nature. And in *Brutopia* Cecilia exposes herself to the risks of insanity or violent death in her ruthless relationship with Henry VIII. What lies behind the idea of catastrophe is the sense of other varieties of the self repressed or obscured by politics, social convention, or simple fear. Bradshaw's journey is ostensibly one of piety—the collecting of her husband's parts—but it leads to acts of outrageous impiety. Savage commits impious acts as the condition of his tour. The will to be whole, and perhaps more than whole, is discovered in opposition to collective sentiment. Dramatically, the technique for summoning the will for this act of persistent rupture consists in constant self-description, the exhortation which found its first expression in a rudimentary form in Billy McPhee's last words in *That Good Between Us.*

Rabey: The most compulsive characters in your recent plays—*Women Beware Women, The Bite of the Night, The Europeans,* and *The Last Supper*—are self-appointed liberators who consciously inflict pain to stimulate. Is the willing of catastrophe on self and others the same as the impulse to tragedy?

Barker: The tragic resides in the refusal of the individual to leave the personality unexcavated, the eruption of will into areas of social piety. Savage's painful expression of secret thought, and the act contingent upon it, bring both him and Helen into the tragic arena. On the other hand conventional tragedy demands punishment for transgression—mental disorder or death. It is the revenge of the collective upon the savage ego. Savage is not punished, at least not by the collective, and Starhemberg defies the collective to the end, drawing Katrin with him. So these plays are not tragic but catastrophist. The tragic denouement, the restoration of discipline over self by society or deity, seems to be in Shakespeare a neutered thing, a watery agency without vigour, unfelt and unbelieved. The punishment Savage receives is terrible loneliness, the effect of knowing too much. Starhemberg and Katrin discover new life through a love that can only be discovered in the extreme of resistance. As with Livia and Leantio, their claim on each other is conditional on rejection of reconciliation with the state. Lvov dies, but then he wishes to.

Rabey: A recurrent theme in your work is the body, its mutilation and forcible mutation by self and others; Helen wonders 'What joint or knuckle, what pared-down shredded section would be the point at which your love would say stop, **essential Helen?**' The drive to discover how much can be done to the human body before it ceases to be desirable, talismanic or powerful emerges as unsettlingly vital. The transgression of ostensible physical limitations and ideals breaks, by association, conventional socially restrictive notions of beauty, desirability, and endurance. For example, in *The Europeans* Starhemberg's ruthless adoration of Katrin leads him into rebellion against the aesthetic ideal of beauty which sends shockwaves into the state's ideal of order.

Barker: The body as conventional ground for controlled desire is one of the undeclared cornerstones of the state. It is inevitably associated with youth, especially with fertility, and effectively locates sexual charisma at the shallowest point. The freedom that some of my characters discover in locating sexual power in the frame of experience, e.g. pain, relates desire to the interior life rather than in the skindeep fascination of the icon. Helen of Troy is described by Homer and all who follow him as youthful, beautiful, impossible-to-see-without-desire, etc., and Helen herself as reluctant, the victim of her appearance, and so on. But we know beauty has nothing to do with desire, and that a beautiful woman cannot launch a thousand ships, whereas we suspect a desirable woman might. This distinction is at the crux of *The Bite of the Night*. The state depends for its continuation on the cult of family and fertility, and fetishizes it by its collusions with the propagation of the beautiful, as thing to be possessed, as body owned and sold. I emphasized this in *Women Beware Women,* but also showed Sordido's ravishing of Bianca as the reverse of the coin. In *The Europeans* Katrin's atrocious condition is a spur to desire in Starhemberg, her eroticism lying precisely in her impossible-to-assimilate history. She has none of the functions of fertility, being unable to feed an infant. By loving Katrin Starhemberg publicly breaks the silent contract of socialized love.

But the body as locus of abuse and fetishization goes back earlier than these plays, certainly to *The Love of a Good Man*. The state has always played fictional games with the flesh of the dead. The Unknown Warrior is a response to the phenomenon of incomprehensible slaughter in the twentieth century, and designed to be an anonymous representation of sacrifice. In other words, the annexation of the innocent for the purposes of the state. I examined this proposition from a number of angles in the play. The symbolic and the actual coincide in the games played around the identity of a single corpse in the midst of monumental mourning. On the other hand, the state's ferocious dismembering of its enemies is of course the motor to *Victory*. The personal ache to recover the murdered, euphemistically called 'The fallen' in the Great Wars, but the 'criminal' after Great Revolutions, reaches its apotheosis in Bradshaw's theft of her husband's head from the sleeping monarch, who transports it about with him, a more powerful talisman than the works hatched inside it. This hypnosis induced by the presence of the body defies rationalism, as we can see in the supreme obscenity of Lenin's tomb. While you are a useful pretext for social policy your body is mummified. As soon as you are discredited, your remains are attacked. Stalin was turfed out of his mausoleum. His flesh had to be abused as well as his ideas. And this in the super-rational society.

Rabey: *Women Beware Women* and *The Europeans* depict speculative, disruptive actions which defy the sentimentalities of false democracies; these actions attack the ideal of 'kindness' by which populism discourages completeness of the self and the individual's will to know the true nature of his or her desires.

Barker: I have tried to open the idea of kindness to examination because it is so frequently employed as a ban on action, a means of stifling will and self-expression. There is a form of kindness which is nothing to do with 'kind' at all, but is a relentless charity which distorts the nature of the doer. Thus to be kind to one's relatives might be to stunt oneself, to be kind to the weak might stunt the ability of the weak to develop their own strategy and so on. Kindness becomes a form of oppression, enabling us to refuse courses of action on the grounds they might injure others. Against this regime of delicacy, Livia's ruthless setting of Sordido on Bianca in *Women Beware Women*, and Starhemberg's despatch of Concilia in *The Europeans* are acts of calculated violence which are creative to both the perpetrator and the ostensible victim. I have tried in *Brutopia* to look for a creative form of kindness in the person of Cecilia. She looks for a truthful form of it, declaring she cannot find kindness in the company of the kind, knowing as she does her father's kindness to be the fake virtu of a Renaissance egotist. More was, in his political relations, a most unkind man, vituperative and merciless, whose Utopia is socialized oppression based on sexual abstinence.

Rabey: In *The Last Supper,* Lvov is an incarnate offence to populism in his completeness of self, when populism promises the provision of so-called 'essential' complimentary elements and contexts which prove to be debilitating, intoxicating and addictive. I'm reminded of Nietzsche's identification of the herd instinct and its enshrined apotheosis in religion. You also seem fascinated by the promises

74

and images of religious faith.

Barker: Lvov creates a religion out of denial, insisting always on returning responsibility to the individual seeker. He is never placatory and rarely congratulatory, making independence of self the first condition of freedom. He plays two versions of kindness against each other, knowing that only by repression are we able to perform acts of social kindness, whereas only by acts of self-affirmation do we achieve the other sort of kindness, truth to character. The persistent acts of rupture be performs with public morality entail an isolation from alternative sources of power. It is paramount for Lvov that he will not play the messiah to those seeking simple moral consolations; the officer asks for a pacifist lecture and goes away empty-handed, as does the farmer, a sinner whose sin we never learn. At the end of the play, the returning officer, hardened and revolutionary, declares that those will be punished who did not make their messages clear—the first priority of power being the unambiguous repetition of moral postures.

I am less interested in writing exposures of religion than in describing the constant swing between submission and independence that religion generates. Sloman, after attacking Lvov for his refusal of democracy, cannot resist the man's sheer self-assertiveness, which he finds immaculate, and after a collective act of cannibalism it is he who asserts the unity of all who have participated. It is Sloman who is the potential high-priest of the cult. Thus his 'Hold hands!' is both a cry of solidarity but also of mutual enslavement. The accommodation which the individual is prepared to make to sustain faith is inordinate, a kind of longing for servitude of mind, and this can be observed in the great rationalist religions also. When Gisela is brutally exposed to bad sex by Lvov, an attempt to break her loyalty, she manages to turn her very proper anger into a controlling pity for him, and it is a source of bitter frustration to him that he cannot break their will to servitude. But the best religious figures are those who are essentially corrupt, and

75

know their corruption. As Stucley declares in *The Castle,* what help can the perfect be to the imperfect? Only the imperfect can help the imperfect.

Rabey: Whereas populism seeks to impose restrictive definitions of the self, the polar opposite force might be desire, which challenges even the *self-defined* limits of the self in a surge of derationalising intuitive legitimacy, a liberation available to all yet defying generalisation.

Barker: Passion destabilizes the character, and by extension, the social cohesiveness of the polity. It is literally incapacitating, which was why it has been regarded as an infliction or a sickness. But desire, reciprocated, directs energy and makes transformation both internal and external. Thus Ann and Skinner together can move mountains (*The Castle*) but Skinner alone becomes a monument to defiance, strenuously powered and a subject of desire in herself, who has no access to desire any more. The cult of Skinner and her wound, her terrible absence, lends her the prospect of real political power, but it is a sterile thing compared to her original state. On the other hand, there is something condemned about Ann's hunger for Krak, and his own dissolution in it. It is unequal and ill-fitting, and its cruelties are not creative in the way that say, Starhemberg's are in *The Europeans*. In all the relationships of desire in my work up until *The Bite of the Night* there is a stronger and a weaker element, whether it's Ann's weakness vis-a-vis Skinner or Leantio's vis-a-vis Livia. But between Helen and Savage there is a relentless and ferocious drive that finds a mutual inspiration, an inevitable passage of destruction.

Rabey: It strikes me that impulses to severance are crucial to your work—demanding the courage to act on one's love or hatred, or, most disturbingly, one's inextricably mingled love *and* hatred.

Barker: 'Impulses to severance' is a good phrase, raising once again the spectre of self-inflicted pain as a means to new knowledge, and yes, the hurt done to a loved one—and by extension, to oneself—is the supremely catastrophic example. This is difficult to articulate. It is near to the subject that occupies much of my attention as a writer, the nature of the bad spirit, the meaning of wickedness. The rupturing of conventional pieties is a common theme in my work—Savage's murder of his father in *The Bite* (it is technically a suicide, but Savage demands it), Orphuls' killing of his mother in *The Europeans,* Cecilia's ecstasy in her father's death in *Brutopia,* all of them gateways to self-development but also appalling and traumatic. There is an earlier form of this in Bradshaw's conscious dehumanization of her son in *Victory.* What the characters do in rupturing these bonds is to create morality for themselves, as if from scratch. They insist on a carte blanche, however impossible. It is as if they were seeing their own lives as theatre, and demanding the right to invent themselves.

Rabey: The simultaneous co-existence of love and cruelty, or desire and pain, in your work is a more complex theme than can be encapsulated in the simplistic terms of deviancy, 'sadism' and 'massochism', in which social notions of deviance have their own effects of oppressive cultural (non-) legitimization. Lvov describes love as 'doing the undoable'. How might we distinguish love from desire?

Barker: To take the first part first, you are correct to expose terms such as 'sadism' and 'massochism' as attempts to bolster a spurious normality in sexual relations. Not all acts of cruelty between lovers can be interpreted as sadism unless a real hatred of the other, as opposed to the profound resentment that lies at the root of desire, is the source of it. By resentment I intend this—the anger, and even shame, felt by the partner in the presence of the inextinguishable power of the other's sex—the spectacle of endless servitude (and ecstasy is a servitude) that sexual power (i.e. sexual difference) lays before us. This is a landscape of hunger which (like cunt in Krak's futile drawings) has neither edge nor width, and forever entails the abolition of dignity and even self-knowledge in the birth and rebirth of wanting.

77

This resentment at servitude lies in the heart of wanting itself, and produces the ambiguous sense of despair and fascination which might lead to violence, a violence shared by both parties. Now, this is nothing at all to do with De Sade's monotonous savagery, where the orgasm is the single end of all imagination, and the attainment of orgasm an ever-diminishing prospect, available only by further refinements of cruelty. De Sade's violence is never mutual—it is not shared pain, but infliction.

The word love is not uncommon in my work, but I only edged towards a meaning for it in *The Europeans,* which is subtitled 'Struggles to love'. And here it is in many ways not mediated through the body as desire is. What Starhemberg does for—and also against—Katrin is to insist on her right to self-description, resistant to the categories invented for her by the state and refusing the false reconciliations of History on the one hand, or parenthood on the other. His love for her is a love for her completion, her pursuit, which he perceives and perhaps judges more finely than she does herself. This certainly involves 'doing the undoable'.

Rabey: The Power of the Dog's subtitle, 'Moments in History and anti-History', seems your first step towards identifying a mythic power in individual pasts as opposed to national pasts. This power is increasingly identified with sexuality in your work, particularly in *Women Beware Women* and *The Breath of the Crowd,* which highlight exposure and realisation of the unlived life, the uniqueness of each personal testimony and the sense of cumulative power involved in sexual encounters.

Barker: There is little or no aperture in *The Power of the Dog* for celebration or the catalogue of restorative things that are commonly associated with the humanist theatre. But what it does assert is the capacity of individuals for alternative experience and private history, which both dives under and is swamped by collective politics. In a world of Historical Method, blunderingly performed by Stalin with materialist rhetoric, an alternative fetishism is created by the

78

dislocated, a viable private madness in collective madness. The image of Ilona, fashion model and atrocity-addict, is not easily prised open by psychological or political interpretation. She is a self-invention of the historical moment, absurd and yet powerfully evocative of wrong-rightness. In this, the play prefigures *The Possibilities,* which are all approaches to the idea of wrong-rightness. They are amoral plays, but powerful assertions of human imagination at the moment when reconciliation is a greater disaster than extinction itself. The willed creation of private history, (Ilona's collection of photographs), its resistance to world-historical forces, (an appalling category if there ever was one) and its insistence on private perception at all costs (she will continue with her narcissism no matter what the objective conditions) comes yet more defiantly in *The Europeans* where atrocity itself, as personified in Katrin, refuses to submit to absorption into historical material (the dead, the executed, the unknown warrior, the fallen, etc.). Katrin is the Screaming Exhibit, a phenomenon that rocks the Museum of Reconciliation. In all these plays, and as you indicate, in *The Breath of the Crowd,* sexual history is made between characters with an authenticity that cannot distinguish their political actions. The dignity that is discovered in this struggle even lends a quality of beauty to the otherwise wholly disreputable. I'm thinking of Scadding in *Downchild,* for example.

Rabey: Your characters insist on absolute truthfulness, in self and others, in sexual relations, however harrowing the consequences. For example, Skinner in *The Castle* tells Ann to leave nothing out of her description of her relations with Krak, 'If I know all I can struggle with it, I can wrestle it to death...' Thus Skinner seeks relief from the self-torturing fascination of 'the imagined thing', which gnaws her to madness.

Barker: The demand for absolute truth in the sexual relationship is simultaneously the key to Skinner's elevation to semi-divine status and a kind of emotional death. The truth is the devastation of hope. In a state of hopelessness she acquires the will to catastrophic experience, passing from passionate love-life to adamantine stoicism. As long as Ann remained untruthful, the possibility of reconciliation existed, though as a sort of half-life, the wanting in pursuit of the unwanting. But by submerging herself in scalding pain, (the very last detail of infidelity) Skinner sheds a defunct self, a dead skin, and even seems to regard sexual madness as nearly comic, when Krak exposes his loss of self to her, his bewilderment in the state of passion.

Rabey: Don't Exaggerate, a direct address to the audience, seems a crucial development in locating obligation in the theatre audience on the specific occasion of performance. The prologues of *The Bite of the Night* and *The Last Supper* similarly emphasize the importance of what the witnesses choose to bring to, and give to, the theatrical experience.

Barker: The importance of *Don't Exaggerate* in my theory of theatre lay in its employment of contradiction and digression as means of returning the onus of moral decision to the audience. I now believe in the de-thronement of the audience, the abolition of its judgemental character, and the assertion of the stage over the auditorium. By this I mean the restitution of power to the actor, not as demonstrator of a given thesis, but as the figure who encourages the audience to abandon its moral and intellectual baggage and permit itself the greater freedom of an imaginative tour, essentially a de-stabilising experience. The proposition of a moral posture, and its immediate demolition, ('You exaggerate! You do exaggerate! You know you do') has the effect of loosening ideology, implying the absence of objective truths, and forcing the audience to make its own decisions about the actions shown or described. What the audience is given, its reward for this dangerous exposure, is beauty, (truth having been annexed by political or psychological theory). *The Last Supper* is beautiful in language and form (I am thinking particularly of the parable entitled 'The Obscure Origins of Domesticity'), whilst being wholly unideological. The play is no longer a proposition about politics at all, though it is certainly about freedom. Rather it is a journey without maps and without clear instructions to the audience, which is sometimes pained by the absence of hidden orders ('Detest this character', 'See the manipulation here', etc.), especially when the character himself lacks stability (Ella in this play is both without words, then highly articulate, and Marya's contradictions are only superficially madness—they are in fact perfectly commensurate with frustrated dominance). In all my work after *Don't Exaggerate* the audience is unable to withdraw into the security of known moral postures. This alone serves to eliminate 'entertainment' from their experience, since entertainment is impossible without very firmly drawn demarcations.

Rabey: *Scenes from an Execution* dramatizes how 'artists have no power and great imagination. The state has no imagination and great power'. Do you think this relationship is essentially antagonistic, one describing the limitations of the other's reach and reference?

Barker: It seems to me impossible that the state and the artist should enjoy anything but a fleeting similarity of interest, usually in the aftermath of a revolution when the artist mistakenly believes his imagination will be licensed as part of the cultural rebirth of a new order. The rapid restitution of economic and social priorities and the assertion of the collective, or its mediators, over the individual interpretation of society, make this inevitably short-lived. States are mechanisms of discipline, and perpetually involved in re-writing and re-ordering experience, annexing it and abolishing it in the interests of proclaimed moral certitudes. The artist, as long as he is in profound union with his imagination, inevitably finds himself opposing ideological imperatives and exposed to censorship. This censorship will always take the form of 'protection' of sensibilities (the weak, women, virtue, the family, our past, etc.) no matter what the ostensible pretensions of the

81

regime—a left regime has to protect 'class' and 'reason' as well as all the rest, and is likely to be more restrictive than certain inert reactionary ones. Women have to be protected against abuse, and the family against its perpetual, but never total, dismemberment. The state is a mass of fictions held together by superior power. I believe this has been the case as long as the state has existed. The problem is to judge which fictions are necessary ones.

Rabey: How might the compulsion of audiences to witness transgression, as depicted in Jacobean drama, and your own, be distinguished from voyeurism? Can the stage release, as well as depict, the unlived life?

Barker: All descriptions and propositions of and about life in drama entail the possibility of imitation. But my plays do not operate as models of behaviour, recommendations or exhortations. They are not pathways out of collective life or manuals of mayhem. They do not attempt to demonstrate wrong life or detail paths to self-knowledge. Every play is provisional, just as every statement must be provisional. I have nothing to teach anyone. In any case, the pain and despair experienced by my characters hardly invite imitation, though conversely, there is no tragic denouement which reinforces the existing moral consensus. Rather the plays remove, plank by plank, the floor of existing moral opinion in order to plead other, unarticulated causes. The audience (if there is such a thing, and since I do not seek a solidarity here, I ought to talk of individuals) feels itself bereft (and frequently exhilarated as a consequence) of its usual critical or empathetic equipment, and even insecure in its laughter, which is the last refuge of uncertainty. But this disarray is not sterile. Since there is a distinct absence of moral convention, the transgressor is not punished, the audience is obliged to arrive at its own judgement, not of situations it knows, but of ones it does not. What occurs in my plays is only partly life as it is known, after all. Mostly, it is unknown life. The audience is stirred at a subconscious level by the sheer volume of imagined life which the actors present. This is not voyeuristic, since it is not a fetishism around an observed action which leaves the witness transfixed but still hermetically sealed in his own moral posture. The possibility that is unlocked in the relations between characters drags the idea of hidden life into the forefront of consciousness. It is an acutely painful, and a half-reluctant experience, to which individuals frequently return.

Rabey: When surrounded by normative systems of predictions, connecting with further normative systems of predictions, rather than with lived experience, one is in danger of being enmeshed in a climate of accrued debilitation—to quote *Don't Exaggerate,* 'the liars operate in the imagination, too'. But the subversive power of the imagination, and its address to an unwontedly full sense of human integrity, might reside in its unpredictability. In discovering integrity in action, the individual invents freedom for himself or herself in a non-ideological way, and becomes answerable to nothing and no one for validation. How close is this to the spirit of enquiry at work in *The Possibilities* and to your sense of theatrical surprise in general? Do the subversive powers of both comedy and tragedy lie in their demonstrations of essential incongruity? Is the vital essence of theatre a power of dislocation?

Barker: The hidden purpose of much modern drama has been the exposure of wrong life. The play states more or less overtly 'beware not to live like this', or in an age of ideology, 'you must put an end to this'. Both comedy and the sorts of tragedies we variously encounter conspire in this missionary intention. And it would be absurd to pretend audiences do not hunger for this instruction as vehemently as writers long to provide it. It is theatre's old obeisance to certain governing conventions. When the play fails to provide instruction in wrong life, unease is created and frequently, a piqued resistance. In *The Possibilities* I persistently refuse the answer an audience anticipates from the predicated situation. There is an element of frustration in it,

83

but what prevents the witnesses of the plays from becoming vociferous in their unwilling subjection to the wholly unpredictable nature of the pieces is the peculiar, simultaneous ecstasy of recognizing the appalling strain of being human. They are not led or instructed by the story. The onus of dealing with the pain is theirs. There is no right course, or wrong action in *Kiss My Hands* or *The Philosophical Lieutenant*. Nor is there a generalized protest at the way we are, or our unkindness to each other. The audience suffers this, but the pain is somehow positive. It can only be that out of the deepest exploration of pain, unmediated by ideology or morality, a certain strength is lent by performance. The power of these pieces in production reveals the meaninglessness of the notion of 'pessimism' in art. It is not pessimism at all, it is the excoriation of experience.

Rabey: I know you resist sentimental or intoxicating celebratory invocations of 'community' such as some would identify as the characteristic cohesive effect of the theatrical experience—the descent (or imposition?) of communality which Hilton and others worship in mystical terms. Rather, you've emphasized the individual reflection of the single audience member, concentrating and witnessing in the darkened stalls. But what then is his relationship to his fellow spectators, and to what extent is this salient to the theatrical experience?

Barker: Yes, I am against the solidarity of the audience. It is easily manipulated and frequently, albeit unconsciously, authoritarian. The best moments in theatre for me are those in which solitary movements can be discerned, in which a sense of contest can be registered between the stage and the disjointed audience. These solitary contests are of course determined by the fact of the existence of others, they would be harder to achieve in isolation. The tension created by an assumed collectivity of response, which then disintegrates, leaving individuals exposed to the effects of actions on the stage, is to me a valid condition of experiencing art. The audience has to sense its moments of division as well as its moments of unity, which I would not deny, though I wouldn't locate this unity in the usual places, perhaps. The unity should surprise as much as the disunity. Often this sense of isolation is affirmed by the light of the foyer, where the normal buzz of the consensus is replaced by a wariness to articulate what is still undigested. But I do not intend the individual to be without a guide. I come back to the actor, who by sheer bravery becomes the focus of hope and the source of security that cannot, in my work, be found in the usual forms of the message or the verisimilitude. In the actor's courage, the audience individual finds his own.

The Offer, the Reward, and the Need to Disappoint

In the old theatre, the actors offered the play as a salesman displays his product—unctuously and with fake gentility. The prologue was the patter of the potentially unemployed. Thus the audience became customers, whose satisfaction was the necessary end of the performance.

In the new theatre, the audience will offer itself to the actors. It will relinquish its status as customer and abandon its expectation of reward. When it ceases to see itself as customer, it will also cease to experience offence.

The reward is a relic of the market place. The old theatre pretends to reward its audience for its effort of attendance, its effort at concentration, its surrender of futile time. You must reward the audience, say the poor critics. Why? Is theatre so intolerable? Is art not necessary for itself? The contrary is the case. It is a privilege to witness art. It is a privilege to hear good actors. In the new theatre there will be no reward because there will be no deal, no swop, or compact. The new theatre will not perceive itself as product. The audience will enter the new theatre out of necessity. In this condition, which is the compulsion of a spiritual hunger, it will cease to pass facile judgements on the play.

To escape the pernicious memory of the market place, the new theatre will dethrone its audience. The audience will no longer sit in tiers. It will not be encouraged to think itself a jury, obsessively judgemental. The actor will dominate the audience, not only by his performance, but also by his elevation above the audience. The audience is not to be rendered uncomfortable, nor attacked. We are not seeking a theatre of massochism. But it must be delivered from the shallowness of its expectations, its appetite for rewards. This narcissistic frisson is a relic of the exchange-relation, and of cultural infancy.

The infantile notion of the reward, which still dominates the serious theatre, is based on critical clichés. The audience feels the reward if it senses the play's 'importance'. Infantile critics are forever in search of 'important' plays. The important play cannot exist however, without denying its own importance. This is because to be recognized as such it must trade in the very cultural, political and social conventions that constitute the discourse of the world *outside* the theatre. In other words, it replaces, reorganizes, or re-perceives the elements of existent ideology. It could not avoid or demolish these without sacrificing its 'importance'. The play that fails the test of 'importance' is invariably felt to be disappointing. The Disappointing play refuses to gratify the audience's thirst for social and political repetition. It robs its audience of the grotesque satisfaction of identifying its enemies and celebrating its prior knowledge—the sickening and secret compact between the author and his audience that distinguishes liberal art.

The Disappointing play squirms away from the notion of 'importance', and instead of offering the reward, delivers the wound. The wound is the aim of the new theatre and the intention of the actor. His performance will create the wound and the wound will be the subject of continuing anxiety. Only anxiety will justify the efforts of the performance. This anxiety will come from the audience's attempt to experience the play outside the confines of ideology. Slowly, the audience will discover the new theatre to be a necessity for its moral and emotional survival. It will endure the wound as a man drawn from a swamp endures the pain of the rope.

The Audience, the Soul and the Stage

When did you last hear a laugh which was
Not a spasm of intoxication
Not a gesture of solidarity
Not a gurgle of vanity
The choral assent of intellectual poseurs but
The irresistible collapse of words
Before the spectacle of truth?

I never have

(Don't Exaggerate)

To discuss the practical or theoretical nature of a contemporary theatre it is necessary to begin from the state of public knowledge. Only from a judgement regarding the state of public knowledge, its sickness or its vitality, can the necessary forms of theatre be deduced.

The Theatre of Catastrophe takes its form from the following assessment;

> That information is a universal commodity
>
> That knowledge is forbidden
>
> That imagination has been maimed by collectivist culture
>
> That in this maiming the public itself has colluded
>
> But that this collusion is nevertheless detected and is experienced as shame

The Theatre of Catastrophe addresses itself to those who suffer the maiming of the imagination. All mechanical art, all ideological art, (the entertaining, the informative) intensifies the pain but simultaneously heightens the unarticulated desire for the restitution of moral speculation, which is the business of theatre. The Theatre of Catastrophe is therefore a theatre for the offended. It has no dialogue with

Those who make poles of narrative and character
Those who proclaim clarity and responsibility
Those who ache to delight the audience
Those who think laughter is a weapon of the oppressed
Those who dream theatre tells the truth
Those who insist on the facts
Those who clamour for fantasy
Those who believe in the existence of ordinary people

The Theatre of Catastrophe is rooted in the idea of the soul, not as immortal form, not as a thing immune from damage, but as innate knowledge of other life. In some, this knowledge is nothing more than a cherished hoard of stereotypes (the sea, the sky, the prospect of love). In others, the Soul breaks with all images it senses corrupt or annexed by ideology (harmony, family, the public) and aspires to new forms. The Theatre of Catastrophe addresses those imperatives of the Soul which most writhe under reproduction. It exhilarates. It creates offence, even among the already offended. It does not limit its address to the educated, though it does not honour ignorance. Above all, it speaks a new language, which is to say it believes language to be revolutionary in a culture which degrades language and smears it as elitist. It makes language as luscious and as spiteful as love, of which it is an expression. It abhors reconciliation which is not won at terrible cost. It demands more of its audience than all existing theatre.

The audience of this theatre is in awe of the actor. It is in awe of him because the actor does not pretend to be the audience (a theatre of recognition) but asserts his difference.

He both suffers more, and exposes more, than the audience anticipates. The audience of The Theatre of Catastrophe is not gratified to see its life reflected on the stage. It comes with a single desire—to witness unlived life, which the ideological and the mechanical conspire to conceal. In this, the Theatre of Catastrophe is more painful than tragedy, since tragedy consoles with restoration, the reassertion of existing moral values. The audience is not flattered with hope, but rather lent pain. It is not taught criticism, but honoured with the truth of the absence of truth. It leaves the theatre privileged, but unrewarded. It does not cluck with collective satisfaction, but divided and solitary, it labours with the burden of an art that denies assimilation.

The Humanist Theatre*

We all really agree.
When we laugh we are together.
Art must be understood.
Wit greases the message.
The actor is a man/woman not
    unlike the author.
The production must be clear.

We celebrate our unity.
The critic is already
    on our side.
The message is important.
The audience is educated
    and goes home
        happy
         or
        fortified.

*First published in "Théâtre en Europe", 1989.

The Catastrophic Theatre

We only sometimes agree.
Laughter conceals fear.
Art is a problem of understanding.
    There is no message.
The actor is different in kind.

The audience cannot grasp
everything; nor did the author.
    We quarrel to love.
The critic must suffer like
    everyone else.
The play is important.
The audience is divided
    and goes home
        disturbed
         or
        amazed.